GOLAZZO
THE FOOTBALL ITALIA YEARS

Jonathan Grade

ISBN 9798697783634

Dedication

For Bertie, Annabel, Sophia and Gabriel

CONTENTS

“4”-WORD

I was in the car. My father was driving us through the streets of Chelsea. It was early summer in 1992 and my school days had thankfully finally just come to an end. While I was deep in thought about the upcoming European Football Championships, my father turned to me and said he had some great news.

“Channel 4 have bought the rights to show Italian football. I know the boss. I’ll see if I can get you some work experience on it over the summer.”

At the time I had no career plan whatsoever. It sounded good, although I knew nothing about Italian football. I wasn’t a fan. I hated the way they took all the British talent away from these shores and I also despised the fans’ hooligan reputation. Heysel was something I hadn’t forgotten. Watching those distressing scenes when I was 11 had really shocked me and as a mad football fan I resented the British clubs’ ban from European competition. Still, it was a bit of extra money during the holidays. I was going to University in France in October, so it would keep me busy for a few months and earn me a bit of cash.

So, in late June I showed up at the offices of Chrysalis Television in West London, not knowing what to expect. In those pre-internet and email days, I had briefly spoken to the Executive Producer, a man by the name of Neil, who told me to report to reception at 10am and he’d take me up to the office.

I was introduced to two of the producers who looked at this spotty teenager and asked: "Do you know anything about Italian football?"

"Erm... I am a big football fan and I watched the World Cup, so I think I know a few of the players."

"Who do you support?"

"Charlton Athletic," I said. That usually got a good laugh. And once again it did.

"Right," they said, handling me a huge file, "do you know what logging is?"

I had no idea what they were talking about. This was my first job in television. There was a huge box of tapes and an A4 ring binder with all the week-by-week results and scorers from the previous season.

"You see those red numbers on the machines? They're called time codes. What we want you to do is describe the action. It doesn't matter if you don't understand the names – it's got Italian commentary. Just note down the name of the team, that'll do."

The tapes I was looking through were from an Italian show called *Novantesimo Minuto*, which translates as *Ninetieth Minute*. It was an Italian football programme that showed the highlights of all the Serie A matches an hour after the final whistle. There would be a two- to three-minute package of each game, but they would cram in as much as they could into that time, so it was a fairly laborious process! Looking at the file, the results and scorers fascinated me. I couldn't believe AC Milan had gone the entire season unbeaten. Their last game saw them turn around a 2–1 half-time deficit against a team called Foggia to win 8–2! I'd been told Italian football was negative and boring. I quickly realised that wasn't the case.

Studying the file brought back memories of the World Cup that had been held in Italy just two years earlier. I was impressed by the amount of world-class talent who plied their trade in Serie A. It really was the place to be. As well as the entire Italian squad, the Dutch trio of Ruud Gullit, Marco van Basten and Frank Rijkaard all played for champions AC Milan. Inter Milan boasted German World Cup-winners Andreas Brehme, Lothar Matthäus and Jürgen Klinsmann. Juventus had Totò Schillaci and Roberto Baggio, the two stars of Italy's World Cup campaign. Fiorentina had a young Argentinian striker called Gabriel Batistuta who I understood was going to be a huge star. And then there was Lazio – a club I was told that was forever in the shadow of city rivals AS Roma – who'd just signed Gazza.

I had so much fun. As a football fan, I slowly got to understand about the league, the big clubs, the smaller clubs. And it was the passion of the Italian fans – or *tifosi* as they are called – which had quite an impact on me. The colour in the stadia, the flags, flares, scarves – you could see it meant everything to them.

Before long, my time with Chrysalis was at an end and I was off to France. And while I would religiously follow Charlton's up-and-down fortunes over the next nine months, I would watch all the Serie A highlights on French TV. I was becoming fascinated by this league. So, in June 1993 I thought I'd get back in touch with Chrysalis.

"Hello Neil, it's Jonathan. Do you remember me from last summer?"

"Yes of course. How are you?"

"Good thanks; I had a great year in France. I've been following Serie A since I was with you and just wondered if you needed any help ahead of the new season."

"That'd be great, it's going to be busy – can you start on Monday? 10 o'clock? See you in reception."

And with that phone call I was back. The company had an informal dinner in late June to celebrate the first year's coverage of Italian football on Channel 4. I thought I'd let them have a few drinks before asking the question I'd wanted to ask since last summer.

"Neil, as you know I've really enjoyed working with you these last two summers. I just wondered…" – my heart was pounding by now – "would there be any chance of a job?"

The whole table looked at me in bewilderment. Trust me to say something like this in front of everyone. Me and my big mouth.

"Yes. It'd be great to have you on board. The money wouldn't be great but…"

"I'm not bothered by that. Thank you so much!"

And at that moment, in a noisy restaurant in West London, my love affair with Italian football was born.

1

A TOUGH INITIATION

Serie A in the early '90s was the mecca of world football. AC Milan had just won back-to-back European Cups. Serie A clubs won five out of six UEFA Cups. They were successful too in the Cup Winners' Cup.

Italia '90 had seen impressive new stadia, passionate fans and great football. And, for English supporters starved of European football for five years following the Heysel tragedy, the team's run to the semi-finals during Italia '90 had captured the public's imagination. But it wasn't just in England that the team had impressed. Paul Gascoigne's tears in the heart-breaking semi-final loss to West Germany was one of the iconic images of the tournament and European clubs were showing interest in him.

Just nine months later it was Italian club Lazio which agreed an £8.5 million price tag, a world record fee at the time. But the transfer would soon run into difficulties. In the 1991 FA Cup Final between Tottenham Hotspur and Nottingham Forest Gazza committed a brutal foul on Gary Charles in the opening minutes and ruptured his anterior cruciate ligament – an injury so serious that the following season was a write-off.

But Lazio were not going to let that deter them. They were determined to get their man and were prepared to be patient. And in the summer of 1992 the English midfielder touched down at Rome's Fiumicino Airport to start the new chapter in his career.

He wouldn't be the only Englishman in Serie A for the 1992/93 season. Des Walker, who'd also played for Nottingham Forest in that

1991 FA Cup Final, joined Sampdoria – coached by future England manager Sven-Göran Eriksson – for £1.5 million. Both Walker and Gascoigne would be joining a player who'd already made quite an impression in Italy.

David Platt had been signed by Bari a year earlier and had impressed in a struggling side. Platt knew all about the San Nicola stadium, having already played (and scored) there against Italy in the third/fourth place play-off match at the 1990 World Cup. He arrived in the southern city amid much excitement following a £5.5 million transfer from Aston Villa, a record for an English club.

Upon his arrival, Platt talked about having a similar impact for the *galletti* as Diego Maradona had at Napoli. That was always going to be a tall order, but he became a huge favourite with the supporters by watching a game with them in the stands whilst serving a suspension. Platt scored 11 goals from midfield – an impressive tally in one of the toughest leagues in the world – but it wasn't enough to save his team from relegation. When Juventus came in with a £6.5 million bid for the Englishman in the summer of 1992, Bari had no choice but to sell.

So, the 1992/93 season kicked off with three of England's World Cup stars – Platt, Walker and Gazza all plying their trade in Italy – and the *Gazzetta* and *Football Italia* cameras were with them every step of the way. From edit suites in Camden to live transmissions from Channel 4, to presenter James Richardson jetting off to every corner of Italy, this was a completely new experience for football fans in the UK.

So, cast your mind back to the autumn of 1992. With the Premier League launching on Sky, live football on terrestrial television was at a premium. With no top-flight football available, it was either live action from the Football League, or live coverage of the best league in the world.

Back then, Italian football was stereotyped as negative and dull. But there was a revolution taking place in front of our very eyes as the passion, the colour as well as the skill of *calcio* had fans up and down the country hooked. The opening weekend of Sky's first Premier League season saw Nottingham Forest labour to a scrappy 1–0 victory over Liverpool.

That first season of *Football Italia* didn't feature James Richardson at live games. Instead Peter Brackley would be presenting the show from a commentary booth in Central London with a variety of co-commentators, most of whom had played in Serie A. The likes of Ray Wilkins, Liam Brady, Joe Jordan, Luther Blissett and Paul Elliott would all be regulars on the programme.

In Italy, meantime, Channel 4 kicked off with a clash between Des Walker's Sampdoria and Lazio, unfortunately without the injured Paul Gascoigne. He would make his debut a few weeks later ... but *Football Italia*'s debut *was* spectacular.

Under glorious September skies, the Stadio Luigi Ferraris was bathed in sunshine as the two sides shared a six-goal thriller. Lazio's other big signing – striker Beppe Signori – had a game to remember, scoring twice.

The opening day of the season proved what an exciting and unpredictable league this really was. The big guns all struggled. Champions Milan stretched their unbeaten run to 36 league matches as they ground out a 1–0 win over Foggia thanks to an own goal. Inter and Roma both lost – the latter at home to newly promoted Pescara in one of the shocks of the season. Juventus could only manage a 0–0 draw with Cagliari.

So that was the opening day sorted. With the live show complete, it was off to watch *Novantesimo Minuto* – the programme that gave me my first insight to Italian football. It was a show transmitted by state broadcaster RAI, and it delivered a 45-minute package of all the Serie A highlights. The presenter in Rome, a larger-than-life character by the name of Giampiero Galeazzi, had previously represented Italy at rowing during the 1968 Olympics.

It took quite a while to get into the swing of logging the matches as they came in, with the footage being edited fairly ruthlessly. On average, you would get about seven or eight seconds for each incident! When the show was over, I'd deliver the tapes from our live match, along with the recordings of *Novantesimo Minuto*, as well as all the other tapes I'd delivered at the start of the day and have them transported to our facilities house in North London. It was now all systems go for a busy week on the *Football Italia* production.

It kicked off on Monday as my employers Chrysalis were contracted to produce a one-hour highlights show for RTÉ, the Irish state broadcaster. For this programme we would show extended highlights of a second match that had taken place at the weekend and not our main live game. The rest of the show would be a round-up from the other eight matches. Our editor, Mike Cross, would be raring to go – always before the 8.00am start time – and the first two hours would be spent editing the roundup or, as we called it, the "goals package".

In later years, at 8.30am we would get a ten-minute satellite feed of the Sunday evening game, which was cut in a similar style to *Novantesimo Minuto* and would sometimes miss out important details, such as a red card or a bad injury that needed reporting.

Once the goals package was completed, the tape would be handed to one of our producers who would work with commentator Gary Bloom and script the matches together ready to be voiced after lunch. Gary would also be provided with extensive commentary notes as he would later on be commentating on a 40-minute edit of whatever the match was that week.

It was a well-oiled machine. While the scripts were being written in our tape library, the bulk of the programme was being edited upstairs. So, shortly after lunch, Gary would commentate on the main match and would have a quick break before voicing the goals package.

By 5.00pm everything would be complete, ready to play out to RTÉ in Dublin. Meantime, 6 miles away in West London, running orders were being put together for *Gazzetta*'s debut in five days' time.

While the production team were busy liaising with James Richardson about the week ahead, there was the opportunity for members of staff working on other productions to earn a credit for the show by suggesting a "buzz word". These were mini-captions we put on the opening part of the show with images behind them that described each segment with a witty tabloid-style headline. Examples for James Richardson's newspaper review would be "page boy" or "between the sheets", and if we were doing a feature on the Rome derby it might be "eternal glory". This whole concept kept Chrysalis' employees highly entertained.

In the first season *Gazzetta* would have a fairly structured format. With the goals package all having been edited and voiced on Monday, these would be inserted straight into the show and there would also be other regular features. Gazza would be interviewed and tell us all about his week and sometimes we might hear from David Platt and Des Walker too. But Gazza was the constant, some weeks he would do a light-hearted and sometimes hilarious sketch with presenter James Richardson to kick off, and we would later on have a five-minute chat with him at any one of numerous locations in Rome – his house, a café, Lazio's training ground, sometimes even in his car! During international weeks we would sometimes interview him in London.

One of the most popular features on the show was James' newspaper review. It was an iconic memory that people still talk about today whenever you mention *Gazzetta*. He would be in some classy Italian café, not only in Rome but he could pop up anywhere in Italy. Milan, Florence, Turin, Naples, Venice, Verona, Bologna, Sardinia, Sicily ... you name it, he'd be there. And he wouldn't just be presenting ... that was only part of it. He would be accompanied by a great pile of Italian newspapers and an enormous ice cream. He would then run through some of the big stories of the week interspersed with some lighter ones. It could be transfer news, fans rioting at the training ground or some highly entertaining behind-the-scenes story.

But there was another ingredient added to *Gazzetta*: Kenneth Wolstenholme – voice of the 1966 World Cup Final – was signed up.

"They think it's all over ... It is now" is possibly the most talked-about commentary line in the history of British sport and Chrysalis wasted no time in employing Ken for the *Gazzetta* voiceover. The great man's impact was huge. It was seen as a massive coup to bring one of the doyens of football voices out of retirement.

But the show didn't just come together. Communication would be continuous between London and Rome as the programme's producers were in constant dialogue with James; working out his schedule for the week, setting up interviews for features, working on his scripts together to make sure his links and news stories were as entertaining as possible. And with his schedule mapped out for the week, everything would be in place for James to send down all his material on a satellite feed late on Thursday evening. On an international weekend James would come to London and bring the tapes himself and in later years a member of the production team would fly out to Italy and bring them back, as this would actually work out cheaper than booking a satellite feed.

There were more than a few dramas on filming days. A group of Fiorentina fans once smashed up the crew's car (it had a Rome numberplate) after Lazio had stolen a point late on in Florence. We also had the police on to us in later years as they clamped down on filming in the sacred Piazza del Duomo in the centre of Milan. There were some great days too, filming links aboard boats in Venice and Sardinia as well as all around Italy as the viewers got a real flavour of the country on a weekly basis.

On a personal level things would gather pace as we headed through the week; when we reached Thursday I would be at my busiest. It was "shot finding" day for our VTs for the live game which (as well as *Gazzetta*) was going to be edited on Friday. I also wanted to get ahead with shots for the various features that would be cut the next day. The words "music piece" would fill me with dread; if one was required for say, a player feature, it'd mean dozens more shots needed ... with Italian coverage the way it was I'd be spooling through tapes for hours. Sometimes I'd be working into the early hours because often there were interruptions.

These mainly consisted of dubs of Serie A footage for various companies, but mainly for the *Fantasy Football League* show and ITV Sport. We had a very good relationship with ITV in particular as, in exchange for various Serie A clips, they'd provide us with Champions League highlights for many years for matches involving Serie A clubs.

I would later strike up a deal with Swedish broadcaster TV3 – who in exchange for our live pre-match VT packages on a Sunday would provide us with full match recordings of the night fixture. This was a great improvement on the ten-minute highlights package that RAI had previously given us!

Thursday night would see me stagger home exhausted at midnight or even later, which gave me a few hours' rest before the 8.00am start for the famous *Gazzetta* Friday edit.

Now I didn't join until the second series, but the edit plan was fairly regimented. We had two edit suites, both of which would start at 8.00am. Back then we would be editing on tape so keeping timings as close to the running order as possible was the key.

The main edit suite would be responsible for cutting most of the show and we had a second edit suite cutting features – the news, the main feature, midweek European or Italian Cup highlights. For the first couple of years I would be based down in the bunker, otherwise known as the tape library. We had a good set-up down there – a monitor, a tape machine, a computer, a printer and a telephone, as well as an ever-growing library of tapes, which was my responsibility. I knew where everything was. Match recordings, other programme recordings, tapes with all our elements of the show such as bumpers, stings, wipes, clean effects tapes for audio (as a lot of programmes had Italian commentary mixed in with the crowd noise on them).

The phone would ring. Time to put the bacon sandwich down and spring into action.

"Grado. It's Steve. Right, for the news I want the following shots ... and I want clean shots, no graphics on them and nice big close ups:

Shot of Vialli looking sad
Baggio celebration
Trapattoni close-up barking out orders
David Platt playing for Bari
Capello doing his nut
Beppe Signori's goals from last week
Gazza at training last week
That shot of Roberto Mancini playing with the dog
A couple of Rubén Sosa goals from last season
Some nice aerials of the San Siro
Two Marco van Basten goals from last season

Some nice passionate Fiorentina crowd shots
Totti looking angry (BUT NOT THE ONE WE USED LAST WEEK!)
Napoli conceding a couple of bad goals
Oh, and some nice Zola action from last week."

The list went on and on. And that was just for the news! In those days, there was no chance of emailing Steve to let him know what was on each tape. I would put the timecode and shot description on a sticky note on the tape and put it into a box which would steadily get heavier and heavier. And I would bring up the tapes in dribs and drabs, deliver them and pray to God the phone wouldn't ring for complaints!

Steve was a perfectionist who taught me so much – and he had standards that he expected of me. Finding shots of players in their club's away kit was an absolute no-no and if the shots were anything under four seconds long there'd be a call back with him growling at me! He gave me every opportunity to learn and progress on the production though – and would soon give me my opportunity in the edit suite. I remember my first match edit well as Torino beat Udinese 1–0 with the goal coming from their star striker Andrea Silenzi.

The first month in particular (before I was cutting VTs for our shows) was hard graft. Once all the shot finding was done I would come up and have a quick chat with Kenneth Wolstenholme about football and his beloved Bolton. He would always know how Charlton had got on and ask who we were playing at the weekend. We would be chatting away until another producer would come in. I would soon be heading back downstairs to find some more shots!

In the first year the programme would always finish with a feature on a player or one of the sides taking place in the Sunday live game. Week two of the season would see Lazio take on Fiorentina. We'd have already spoken to Gazza, so there would be a Fiorentina feature to end the show, no doubt featuring their talismanic striker Gabriel Batistuta.

I may have been generally disorganised but I ran that tape library like clockwork. My first day as a full-time employee had seen me ordered to do photocopies of all three log files from the first season! I was at the photocopier for a day – there were A4 ring binders crammed full of log sheets. These labour-intensive tasks didn't deter me though and I made sure all the log files were kept up to date, tapes were labelled and put on the correct shelves, and that they were colour-coded season by season. I put logs in the tape covers to help people if they needed something else from the tape I'd given them. I made sure all the logs for the week were complete well in advance of the *Gazzetta* edit, typed out and printed.

Returning to that *Gazzetta* edit: Ken would kick things off with a bacon sandwich before being given all the scripts and he would voice everything before lunchtime. It would be fairly extensive, voicing the top of the show, the "coming up" and "welcome back" teases, the tables and top scorers and linking into the feature at the end of the show. He then had to voice the scripted VTs for Sunday's live game as well as a goals package we ran at half time featuring the best of the previous week's action. Finally, he then had to voice the top of the RTÉ show and the links for the rest of it. After that he would have his lunch. Avocado salad with prawns, bottle of white wine. He didn't drink it all, well, not most weeks anyway!

So, after the news and the feature had been cut, they would be brought into the main edit and put in the programme. Short features such as Gazza's week would be cut in the main suite and finally, at the end of the day, we would see where we were with timings before editing our "buffer". This was a long edit with commentary of one of the main matches with the purpose of editing it to fit whatever time we had left to fill in the show. And with that we were done.

The final job was being carried out in the other edit as Ken's voice had been put onto a new tape and we would now be editing the VTs for Sunday's live game. Finally, we would all be done and the *Gazzetta* master would be delivered to Channel 4, which would be my job once I was working on the show. In my pre-driving days it at least enabled me to get a taxi home!

There would be about four boxes of tapes from the day, which I'd then bring back down to the library (thankfully there was a lift) and I would leave the tapes there and the *Gazzetta* week was at an end.

Our *Football Italia* live show would soon be upon us though, and with the VTs all assembled on several tapes I would be transporting them home too in an enormous bag from our facilities house which I'd then bring to Channel 4 on Sunday morning.

2

MILAN-EASY

Back in the early '90s AC Milan were the dominant force in football both at home and in Europe. If you talk about that side today people will first of all mention the famous Dutch trio of Gullit, van Basten and Rijkaard. They were just three of a record-breaking number of 73 foreign players – or *stranieri* – plying their trade in the top league in the world and it was Milan who had the pick of them.

There was hardly a weakness in the team. The back four remain club legends. Right back Mauro Tassotti was with the club for 17 years before becoming assistant coach. Centre halves Franco Baresi and Alessandro Costacurta formed an almost impenetrable barrier and along with left back Paolo Maldini they would spend their entire careers with the *rossoneri*. Between them they amassed a whopping 273 Italy caps between them.

Following Arrigo Sacchi's departure from the club in 1991 Fabio Capello was appointed. Sacchi had led the club to back-to-back European Cup victories between 1988 and 1990 and rather like himself Capello was not the most popular appointment. After an almost non-existent playing career, Sacchi had coined the phrase "I didn't realise that in order to become a jockey you had to have been a horse first." However, he confounded the critics to guide the club to glory both at home and in Europe.

Similarly, Capello was not a popular appointment. He was seen as a "yes man" to club President Silvio Berlusconi, but despite this he proved everybody wrong to make the critics eat their words and in some style too. The famous unbeaten 1991/92 season – Capello's first with the club – had made not just Italian but European football sit up and take notice.

Going into Chrysalis' first season of coverage – back in 1992 – Milan were by far and away the best side in Serie A. Bankrolled by Berlusconi, the club were even stronger going into the new season. Jean-Pierre Papin had arrived from Marseille for £10 million and Gianluigi Lentini joined from Torino for a world record £13 million after a much-publicised transfer.

They started the new campaign where they had left off the last. Six straight wins had them setting the pace once again, but it wasn't all plain sailing. They scraped past Foggia on the opening weekend thanks to an own goal. This was a side they'd scored eight against just a few months earlier.

The second weekend of the campaign saw them ship four goals at newly promoted Pescara before they eventually turned around a 4–2 deficit into a 5–4 victory. A midfielder by the name of a certain Massimiliano Allegri was on the scoresheet for the Serie A new boys that day. He'd eventually score 12 times in what was a forgettable return to the top flight for the *delfini*, and despite never playing for any of the big guns in Italy his coaching career would prove to be very different.

Come the start of October, Milan clicked into gear. Facing Fiorentina in Florence in front one of Italian football's most passionate fan bases is always tough, but Fabio Capello's side made a mockery of that as they put their opponents to the sword, scoring seven times in what was a record-breaking Serie A weekend of 48 goals across nine matches. It was Fiorentina's worst ever home defeat in Serie A.

The following week, *Football Italia*'s cameras caught up with Milan. And the timing couldn't have been better as the *rossoneri* remained in top gear for the visit of Lazio. Goals were always on the agenda as these two sides would be the joint top scorers of the season, netting 65 times apiece.

It turned out to be one of the matches of the season. Milan raced into a two-goal lead after strikes from Gullit and Papin. Aron Winter halved the deficit. Two Marco van Basten penalties sandwiched a Diego Fuser rocket. But Lazio wouldn't roll over. Beppe Signori pulled it back to 4–3. Finally Marco Simone sealed the win as the *rossoneri* maintained their 100% start to the season. Serie A had arrived on British screens and the viewers were loving it.

The winning run came to an end just a fortnight later as Torino picked up a point at the San Siro. But it would prove to be a temporary blip as the following week the *rossoneri* hit five in Naples, Marco van Basten grabbing four of them.

Nobody was able to keep up with the blistering pace Milan were setting. Torino were four points back with Inter and Juventus trailing even further behind. With teams being awarded two points for a win back then, that was a lot of ground to make up. Fabio Capello's side hadn't lost for 43 matches!

And next up was the Milanese derby, a match in which Inter couldn't afford to lose any more ground. Gianluigi Lentini's stunning strike put Milan ahead. Inter desperately needed a goal and they got it from the unlikeliest of sources – Gigi De Agostini's tame shot somehow sneaked through the arms of Francesco Antonioli to gift the *nerazzurri* a point and the five-point gap between these rivals remained intact.

Seven days later and another huge test awaited Milan as they travelled to the Stadio delle Alpi to face Juventus. The previous season had seen Juve come closer than anybody to beating Milan. An injury-time own goal by Massimo Carrera in just the third week of the campaign earned Fabio Capello's side a draw. Who knows what might have happened had Juventus clung on?

Twelve months on and the *bianconeri* had made an impressive start to the season. They sat four points behind Milan and were their closest challengers. Only Inter had beaten them in the first ten rounds and they were fresh from a dramatic last-minute victory against Torino in the derby seven days earlier.

Juventus were coached by a legend of the Italian game. Giovanni Trapattoni had presided over a period of great success during his first spell as coach between the mid-1970s and mid-'80s, during which he made history by winning all the UEFA club competitions. It had also been a great period time domestically for Juventus as they won league titles during that time – and after the last of these in 1986 he moved to Inter where things went pretty impressively too, winning the UEFA Cup as well as a league title.

However, his first season back hadn't been as successful. Juventus had finished a distant second to runaway leaders Milan. Juve also reached the final of the Coppa Italia though, but they were defeated over two legs by Parma.

So, in the summer of 1992, Juventus moved to close the gap on Milan by spending big. In came Gianluca Vialli from Sampdoria, English midfielder David Platt from relegated Bari and German international Andreas Möller – he'd arrived in Turin from Eintracht Frankfurt.

Under the watery November sunshine, the top two went head to head. A win would move the home side to within a couple of points of leaders Milan. The match was every bit as tight as predicted. Both sides hit the woodwork before Milan went ahead. A trademark exquisite finish from Marco Simone would ultimately send the *rossoneri* six points clear but the afternoon would end in dramatic fashion as Milan goalkeeper Sebastiano Rossi – on for the injured Francesco Antonioli – saved Gianluca Vialli's penalty. Elsewhere, Inter's dramatic late winner against Brescia would push them above Juventus and into second.

This result would be just the start of a shocking run of form for the Old Lady. Defeat would follow at bitter rivals Fiorentina and then Foggia too, making it three losses in a row and piling the pressure on Giovanni Trapattoni. It left the club's title hopes in tatters. They wouldn't win again until mid-January.

After winning in Turin, Milan were held by Udinese at the San Siro the following week – and while Juventus were lurching from one disaster to the next it was left to Inter to provide some sort of title challenge. The following fortnight though would see the *nerazzurri* having an equally dire time of it themselves.

A humiliating 3–0 defeat in a deluge at struggling Ancona – a team in their debut Serie A season – was followed by a loss to Lazio, as Osvaldo Bagnoli's side conceded six times in just two games. Seven days later, Milan wouldn't make the same mistake as Inter as the *rossoneri* eased to victory over Ancona, and there was no stopping Fabio Capello's side in the run-up to Christmas.

1992 would end as it started with Milan cruising at the top; by now they were eight points clear and had gone a calendar year without a league defeat. Going into 1993 there were two questions to be asked: Could anyone beat them? Could anyone challenge them for the title? The answer, remarkably, was yes on both counts.

It looked like defeat might come in the first game of the New Year after captain Franco Baresi was sent off in the opening minutes at Roma. But as well as having a star-studded attacking line-up this Milan side was made of steel. With Baresi dismissed, plus van Basten and Rijkaard out injured, it was left to the other member of the famous Dutch trio to take centre stage.

Ruud Gullit's explosive volley after half an hour proved the difference as Milan withstood everything the home side could throw at them. If Roma couldn't beat the champions – even with a man advantage for all but the entire match – who could?

Across the capital Roma's bitter rivals Lazio were enjoying an exceptional spell with summer signing Beppe Signori having a dream first season for the club. The forward had joined the previous summer from Foggia for a fee of just £3 million and his two goals against Brescia made it 16 in just 15 matches. He would go on to become Serie A top scorer – or *capocannoniere* – in his debut season in the capital. For English viewers though, it was all about another of Lazio's stars.

Paul Gascoigne was just six months into his Lazio career but there had, as ever, been a multitude of highs and lows. Amid much fanfare September had seen him make his long-awaited Serie A debut for the club – against Genoa at the Stadio Olimpico. And the day was not without its moments of drama. There was a collective intake of breath as the visitors' Mario Bortolazzi brought Gazza crashing to the turf early on but thankfully there was no damage done. The Englishman was withdrawn at half time due to him lacking match fitness as the two sides shared the points.

As the weeks went on, Gazza was playing an increasingly influential role in the Roman club's midfield, impressing players and coaches alike. The one criticism – his "conditioning." As talented as he undoubtedly was, Italy in the 1990s led the way in sport science and diet was a huge part of that. Gazza's weight was monitored regularly by the club's management.

On the field though he was impressing. With Signori regularly on the scoresheet – thanks in no small part to the contribution of a certain Englishman – the club was riding high as they faced the first of the season's derbies with bitter rivals Roma.

There are many cross-city rivalries in Italian football. Milan against Inter. Juventus against Torino. Genoa against Sampdoria. There are even big grudge matches between clubs in different cities. Whenever Juventus meet Inter the match is known as the "derby of Italy". When Roma face Napoli it's the "derby of the south". Fiorentina hold a particular hatred for Juventus after the *bianconeri* clinched the 1982 scudetto on the final day, before some years later signing Roberto Baggio – the darling of the *viola* faithful.

But the bad blood between Fiorentina and Juventus is mainly felt in Florence. Nothing in Italy though quite compares with "*il derby della capitale*". The fact that a Rome derby rarely finishes without a red card is testament to that.

Historically Roma have been the bigger club and enjoyed far more success than Lazio, although that changed towards the end of the twentieth century thanks to the millions invested by former President Sergio Cragnotti. It was a period which saw the club pick up a multitude of trophies both at home and in Europe.

Back in 1992 though Roma were considered the more successful of the two sides. They enjoyed bigger crowds, boasted two Serie A titles to Lazio's one, seven Coppa Italia titles to Lazio's one and had been a whisker away from winning the European Cup in 1984.

Ahead of this derby though it was Lazio in front of Roma in the standings, albeit by just a point. Against a backdrop of stunning colour – red and yellow at one end, sky blue and white at the other – the match kicked off and what followed was 90 minutes of anxiety and tension. Losing was not an option for either set of players or supporters.

The deadlock was broken just two minutes into the second half. Giuseppe Giannini – captain and symbol of his home club – swept the *giallorossi* into the lead. Cue bedlam in the Curva Sud as the Roma fans celebrated as if this was a goal to win a cup final. But the drama was yet to come as Paul Gascoigne chose the perfect moment to give his Lazio career lift-off, and in some style too! His header with four minutes remaining rescued his side from defeat, and the emotion of the moment got to him. It had been two years since Italia '90 and the tears in Turin during England's semi-final defeat to Germany. This time though he was crying in far happier circumstances.

Seven days later Gazza was making headlines again. His stunning solo goal helped Lazio to two points away to Pescara. He was now playing a key role in this Lazio side. The weight issue was still a matter of conjecture for the ever-critical Italian press but his performances on the pitch were impressing players, fans and media alike. It seemed his off-the-field problems were a thing of the past. But the meeting with Juventus in the New Year would see him dropped by coach Dino Zoff due to his "poor physical condition". And post-match all hell broke loose.

The match ended in a 1–1 draw, a result which saw Lazio remain in the top four. After the game, Gazza was asked his opinion on not playing and the reasons for it. His reply? Belching into the reporter's microphone. The Italian media, as well as club President Sergio Cragnotti, went into overdrive. The end result was a £9,000 fine. The fact that he was in press silence endeared him to the club's fans who were asking the question why the media were trying to interview him.

Gazza would go on to make headlines throughout his debut season in Italy, although thankfully post-"burp-gate" it was more for on his on-field performances than his antics off it. He would score against Milan and Atalanta and while the Lazio fans worshipped him, the Italian media were finally warming to him.

After being sent off away to Genoa he took the referee's decision with good grace. No protestation, just handshakes all round, including with the referee. His season ended in fine style with a man of the match performance against Ancona as the side from the capital qualified for Europe for the first time since 1975.

Despite the best efforts of Gazza, Lazio were never really in the title race, where once again Milan looked a class apart. After going unbeaten the previous season, they were still seemingly unstoppable and at the halfway mark had a staggering 31 out of 34 points – a record for an 18-team Serie A.

While city rivals Inter were doing their best to hang onto Milan's coat tails, it was another side from Lombardy who were gaining rave reviews. Atalanta had appointed an unproven coach from Viareggio who was in just his second season in Italy's top flight.

His name was Marcello Lippi and he would go on to achieve remarkable things among some of the bigger names in Serie A, most notably in two spells at Juventus, before winning the World Cup with Italy in 2006. His Atalanta side had already beaten the big trio of Parma, Fiorentina and Roma, and would reach the halfway mark in third place with only the two Milan clubs above them.

Lippi though, in his trademark cautious style, was playing down expectations. "Our first priority is avoiding relegation", would be his standard reply. Atalanta would eventually finish in a highly creditable seventh place.

As for Inter, they were doing their best to keep up with the runaway leaders. Uruguayan forward Rubén Sosa was in a rich vein of form, scoring in the first five matches of the calendar year in what was his first season at the club. But not even he could keep Inter in touch with the *rossoneri*. The *nerazzurri* went six league games without a win and even though they were still Milan's closest challengers the gap was a massive 11 points – in the days of two points for a win, this was surely unsurmountable. In early March though, the title race that had looked to be a foregone conclusion took a dramatic twist.

First Inter won comfortably away to a Juventus side that had collapsed alarmingly in recent months. On the same day, history was made 150 kilometres away at the San Siro as Milan's 58-match unbeaten run was finally ended. A free kick from Colombian star Faustino Asprilla gave Parma a stunning win.

"Capello's fired" was the tongue-in-cheek retort from Milan president Silvio Berlusconi on a momentous day. Not only did Asprilla score a goal of huge significance, but it would launch a career which would be characterised by some explosive goals for Parma.

Suddenly Inter were revitalised. Three straight victories followed and Milan, visibly shaken by the defeat to Parma, couldn't manage a win. The gap at the top was down to seven points ahead of a season-defining second Milan derby.

Ruud Gullit's late equaliser rescued a precious point for the *rossoneri*, but all of a sudden they were struggling. A second defeat of the season soon followed as they were humbled 3–1 by Juventus at the San Siro. On the same weekend, Inter won comfortably in Brescia. What had been a 12-point lead three months earlier was down to just five.

The following weekend Inter comfortably saw off struggling Ancona. Milan were held to a goalless draw at Udinese. Just four points now separated the Milan giants.

At the other end of the table Fiorentina, one of the grandest clubs in the country –winners of two scudetti as well as six Italian Cups – were in freefall, and they were about to appoint their third coach of the campaign.

Gigi Radice had previously been sent packing following a complete breakdown in communications with President Vittorio Cecchi Gori despite the club being second in the table. The replacement was Aldo Agroppi, a coach with limited experience at the highest level. The change proved disastrous as Fiorentina went from being Milan's closest challengers at the top, to crashing towards the relegation zone at a rate of knots.

They failed to win for ten matches as the black cloud hanging over the Artemio Franchi stadium showed no sign of lifting. The club had only ever been relegated from Serie A twice in their proud history but their future in the top flight was in peril. Back then, the bottom four teams were relegated and after losing to Sampdoria in late March only Fiorentina's goal difference was keeping their heads above water. A 3–0 defeat to Juventus signalled the end of Agroppi's disastrous reign, which had yielded just two victories. In came Luciano Chiarugi for the final five games with survival very much on the line.

With Serie A new boys Ancona and Pescara cut well adrift at the bottom, there were two relegation places left and there were some big names down there. Not only Fiorentina but Genoa too – the nine-time Serie A champions were level with the *viola*. Napoli – title-winners just three years previously – were far from safe either.

At the summit though, the season was approaching the business end and things were getting very interesting. With only three games left, Milan held a four-point advantage over Inter and, due to upcoming European Cup commitments, Fabio Capello's side would be playing away to Cagliari two days before Inter took on Foggia at the San Siro.

Despite going a goal down early on, Milan rallied but could only earn a point, thus opening the door for Inter even further. They were at home to a Foggia side in mid-table and with absolutely nothing to play for. Surely the *nerazzurri* would move to within three points of their city rivals? What followed was an afternoon of controversy, recriminations and chaos.

It had all started so well. Rubén Sosa fired Inter into a first-half lead and they seemed home and dry when they were given the chance to go 2–0 up from the penalty spot. But after Sosa had successfully converted, the referee ordered a retake and the Uruguayan missed.

Things went badly wrong for Inter after the interval. First, they were reduced to ten men following Paolo Tramezzani's cynical foul on Andrea Seno. Inexplicably though, the referee issued a red card to Luigi de Agostini to stun the San Siro. To make matters worse, Bryan Roy made it 1–1 in the dying minutes to all but end Inter's scudetto dreams.

So, with just two games to go, Milan were just a point from the title and they got it after another uninspiring performance at home to relegation-threatened Brescia. The title had been won but Milan really had limped over the line. Whether their run to the Champions League Final had anything to do with it, or whether their unbeaten run ending was a factor we'll never know, but just one win in the final dozen games told its own story. Nonetheless, back-to-back titles – and number 13 in all – had been won and what an impact Fabio Capello had made. The coach dubbed the "yes man" had proved the doubters wrong once again.

With the season entering its final round the real drama was at the bottom of the table. Fiorentina started it alongside Brescia in the relegation zone. The *viola* would take on Foggia while Brescia had a home clash with another side going through the motions – Sampdoria. Udinese were just a point ahead but faced the toughest game of the trio away to Roma. Genoa were also not mathematically certain of safety but were against the now out-of-form champions. The 2–2 draw ensured safety for Genoa, but the drama persisted elsewhere.

Fiorentina made a mockery of a run of one win in ten matches to race into a four-goal first-half lead. Brescia were seeing off Sampdoria and Udinese were a goal down in the capital. This meant that it would be Udinese heading down to Serie B. Both Fiorentina and Brescia would be level on points, meaning they'd have to contest a relegation play-off! However, that was to change dramatically…

Foggia pulled two goals back in Florence, which mattered little as they went down to a 6–2 defeat, but there was an eerie silence in the Artemio Franchi stadium as news filtered through that Udinese had equalised in Rome.

That goal would have huge implications – Udinese, Brescia and Fiorentina would now all finish level on points and with Fiorentina having the worst record of the three clubs' head-to-head clashes during the season, it would relegate the *viola* and ensure a play-off between Brescia and Udinese.

Despite having the best goal difference of the three clubs it was the Tuscan giants – Batistuta et al – who would be facing their first Serie B campaign in over half a century. They would be joined there by Brescia after they were defeated 3–1 by Udinese in that play-off match.

Back in London, changes were afoot at Chrysalis Television ahead of the second season on Channel 4. The first year had been a resounding success, both *Gazzetta* and *Football Italia* had attracted rave reviews from fans and press alike (the first match between Sampdoria and Lazio attracting over 3 million viewers) but the feeling was that the coverage could be improved yet further. So, the decision was made to have James Richardson – Channel 4's face of

Italian football – to not only present the *Gazzetta* show but also the live transmission too. Having a presence in the stadium meant we would be able to improve our coverage in several ways.

For a start, *Football Italia* was one of the first live football shows to have commentary not on site; Peter Brackley and his co-commentator were based in the Channel 4 basement and there were several hurdles to overcome during the first season. Getting team news from the stadium was notoriously difficult in those pre-internet and social media days, so by having James in the venue we'd overcome this hurdle. Despite being in London people still believed Brackers was actually in Italy and on more than one occasion he would inform us that his taxi driver at Brighton station would say "Blimey Peter, you got back from Italy quick!"

The other issue we'd experienced in the first season was the coverage. RAI's coverage of Serie A was different to say the least, and there were a few occasions when a major match incident occurred and it was unclear as to what the referee's decision was. We now had a presence in the stadium so James could inform us about what was going on. There were other advantages, too. Because we had our own camera in the stadium, we could provide very basic single-camera coverage in case we lost the feed of the match. This happened on more than one occasion, none more so than in a top-of-the-table clash between Parma and Juventus in 1998, when the side from Turin came from 2–0 down to earn a draw. Their second goal – scored by Filippo Inzaghi – was covered by our camera due to loss of pictures!

Other problems from our Italian friends at RAI cropped up on occasion too. A particularly memorable mishap took place during the clash between Milan and Parma in 1994. As Peter Brackley and Ray Wilkins were describing the action, our coverage suddenly switched to Fiorentina versus Bari, which caused no end of panic in the live gallery and the commentary box. Brackers laughed it off in his own inimitable fashion and thankfully normal service was soon resumed and we returned to the San Siro.

Things were also starting to change in Italian broadcasting. The state broadcaster RAI – who'd held the rights for international broadcasters – had released one fixture per week for Pay TV. That match would be played in the evening, ruling it out for live *Football Italia* coverage. Thankfully in those early days they wouldn't always pick the best game of the week as they were looking to cover as many teams as possible during the first couple of seasons, but that would change further down the line.

After the three-month summer break, *Football Italia* returned to British screens in late August. Off the field there had been plenty of changes ahead of the Serie A kick-off in terms of personnel, most notably with the champions. With the club going for a hat-trick of scudetti, the playing squad had gone through a major overhaul and after a period of unparalleled success it was time to say farewell to their renowned Dutch trio. Frank Rijkaard returned to Ajax, Ruud Gullit surprisingly left for Sampdoria and Marco van Basten's recurring ankle problems meant he wouldn't feature at all during the season or the subsequent World Cup in the United States. It wasn't clear at the time, but he wouldn't overcome his chronic injury problems, and was forced to retire in 1995. The only notable addition was right back Christian Panucci from Genoa for £4.75 million.

Across town it was a role reversal. While Milan had waved goodbye to two of their Dutch stars, Inter signed two others in the shape of Dennis Bergkamp and Wim Jonk, both of whom joined from Ajax. It wasn't just Inter who'd been busy in the transfer market, though. In the capital both Roma and Lazio had strengthened their squads, hoping to close the gap on their northern rivals.

Roma's signing of Abel Balbo from Udinese was a real statement of intent – the Argentine snapped up for £7.7 million. He would go on to become a symbol of the *giallorossi*, scoring 78 goals in his five seasons with the club. He would be playing under new boss Carlo Mazzone, finally in his dream job. Roman born and bred, the veteran coach had just guided Cagliari to European qualification for the first time since 1970 and the heady days of the legendary Gigi Riva.

One of the country's top keepers – Luca Marchegiani – would be joining Lazio from Torino, the £5.6 million fee was a record for a goalkeeper at the time. He would stay in the capital for ten seasons – winning trophies galore along the way in what proved to be a golden era for the *biancocelesti*.

So, the season kicked off and the reigning champions (minus van Basten) would struggle for goals throughout the campaign. The question was would their much-revered defence would be as impenetrable as ever?

The campaign started for them 1,000 kilometres south of Milan at the Via del Mare stadium. Home side Lecce had just been promoted from Serie B and in front of a feverish crowd of 35,000 the champions looked decidedly rusty. Chance after chance went begging in a match the visitors completely dominated before a moment of brilliance from Zvonimir Boban won it. That opener would be an indication of how far out of their depth Lecce were in Serie A in 1993/94. They ended the season with just three wins and a total of 11 points – the lowest in the league's history.

Football Italia kicked off the season in Naples with the visit of Sampdoria and both Ruud Gullit and England's David Platt were in the starting line-up. After a disappointing year with Juventus he'd transferred to Sven-Göran Eriksson's side for £7 million, becoming the lone Brit to play for the club following Des Walker's return home after a fairly unsuccessful year in Genoa.

With James Richardson hosting from the San Paolo stadium, the season got off to a fine start – British viewers were able to see Platt as well as star signing Ruud Gullit score on their league debuts for the club as Sampdoria kicked off with a 2–1 win.

The opening weeks of the campaign would see the top clubs all too inconsistent. Juventus would miss not one but two penalties during their defeat to Roma before putting Sampdoria to the sword in Turin. Roma then followed up their win against Juventus by losing at home to Napoli. Inter would lose at Cagliari. Lazio would beat Parma and then lose to Cremonese.

All were inconsistent ... except for one team. The reigning champions. They won five of their first six Serie A games to once again find themselves at the top of the table. While they weren't prolific scorers, the defence was impenetrable, keeping clean sheet after clean sheet. They actually wouldn't concede at all until their draw at Foggia in week eight, after some 691 minutes!

Gazza, meanwhile, was unfortunately having fitness problems once again. The opening game against Foggia set the tone for a frustrating start to the season as coach Dino Zoff couldn't get 90 minutes out of him and left the Lazio star increasingly frustrated.

Some 500 kilometres north it was a very different story for Britain's other Serie A export, David Platt. He'd found the net four times during the first seven games and had made quite an impact. Along with new signing Ruud Gullit and talent such as the mercurial Roberto Mancini, future Champions League winner (with Juventus) Vladimir Jugović and flying winger Attilio Lombardo, this Sampdoria side was an exciting one to watch.

Swedish coach Sven-Göran Eriksson had joined the club in 1992, just 12 months after the club had won the scudetto. In that first season, he'd guided the *blucerchiati* to a seventh-place finish but after reaching the Champions League final in 1992 (and narrowly missing out to Barcelona in extra time) the fans demanded more ... and they would get it in the Swede's second season.

The 1993/94 campaign would see Sampdoria end up in third place and they were Milan's closest challengers for much of the season, briefly leading the division at the start of November, after beating the *rossoneri* in one of the games of the season. But the best was yet to come.

The Coppa Italia was a much-maligned competition. During the 1990s it never had the glamour of its English equivalent, the FA Cup. All the matches were played in midweek in front of embarrassingly low crowds, although naturally the fans would show more interest if their side progressed to the latter stages of the competition.

In 1994 Sampdoria's cup campaign had some real momentum about it. They'd won the competition three times in the 1980s and this season they'd certainly ridden their luck, surviving two penalty shoot-outs before reaching the semi-finals where they'd face a two-legged tussle with Parma. After winning the home leg 2–1, Sampdoria's place in the final was far from assured but a 1–0 win in the return thanks to Ruud Gullit's stylish finish sent them into the final, where they'd meet the tournament's surprise package, second division Ancona. They were a team that had been relegated from Serie A the previous season but had already beaten Napoli and qualified for the final following a narrow victory in the semi-finals over Torino, the holders.

Back then the final was also played over two legs and the first of these was played at the Stadio del Conero on the Adriatic coast. Ancona were unable to make the most of home advantage as the sides played out a dull goalless draw, meaning it was all to play for in the second leg.

In the early years of *Football Italia*, we ran a goal of the month competition, the prize being an all-expenses paid trip to a top Italian match. There would usually be three or more groups that we would take at various points in the season and as I reached the end of my first year with Chrysalis Television I was asked – along with a work colleague – if I would like to accompany the competition winners to the second leg of the Italian Cup Final. It wasn't a hard decision to make!

So off we all went to Milan where we would take a company coach transfer to Genoa. I had only been to Italy once before, so I had not had much of an insight into this beautiful country. As our coach got closer to Genoa I noticed how the landscape changed dramatically. The flat Lombardy fields were replaced by much more rugged terrain; steep hills, endless tunnels on the autostrada and of course the Ligurian Sea came into view. It really was a beautiful city and great introduction to the country.

Over 40,000 packed out the Stadio Luigi Ferraris on a warm spring evening in late April, a far cry from the sparsely attended early rounds. It was my first taste of an Italian match and an experience I wouldn't forget. As kick-off approached, the Sampdoria ultras unfurled huge blue flags at both ends of the ground. The passion of the *tifosi* (fans) was a completely new experience for me – it was like nothing I had ever seen in the UK.

Once again, the match started as a very tense affair. The tie was still goalless at half time, despite the home fans doing their best to roar their team on from the first whistle – and they were rewarded handsomely after the interval.

After half time Sampdoria – and in particular Attilio Lombardo and Ruud Gullit – tore the Ancona defence to shreds time and again to romp home with a 6–1 victory and earn a fourth Coppa Italia title. Just as importantly, it meant European football for the club once again in the shape of the Cup Winners' Cup.

In Serie A the season was really starting to take shape as Milan travelled to Sampdoria at the end of October for a top-of-the-table clash. Just one point separated the sides on what was an emotional occasion, coming so soon after the passing of the Genovese club's hugely popular president – Paolo Mantovani.

The match would live up to its billing as Milan went 2–0 up in the first half and took complete control. What happened after the break was both sensational and contentious as the champions saw a string of controversial decisions go against them. Salt was rubbed into their wounds when Ruud Gullit grabbed the winner against his former side to send Sampdoria joint top of the table.

It was the first time in over two decades that Milan had lost from being two goals up. Were their dreams of a hat-trick of scudetti looking in serious danger?

The response was emphatic as order was restored seven days later. Goals from Christian Panucci and Jean-Pierre Papin sealed a 2–1 win in the Milan derby – on the same day Sampdoria lost at home to Cagliari and Juventus suffered a 2–0 defeat in Parma. Milan were back on top where they would remain all season.

And Juventus would soon lose further ground. They'd already suffered a huge setback in the second week of the season as star striker Gianluca Vialli fractured his foot – the injury would rule him out until the final weeks of the campaign. A youngster by the name of Alessandro Del Piero would start to break into the first team – the 4–0 rout of newly promoted Reggiana saw the future club legend score for the first time in a Juventus jersey.

After thrashing Genoa at the end of October, Juventus would gain just one win from their next four Serie A games – ruining any chance they had of overtaking pace-setters Milan.

Parma were now Milan's closest challengers – only behind the reigning champions on goal difference – and they looked a different beast to previous seasons. The double signing from Napoli of Massimo Crippa and the impressive Gianfranco Zola was a master stroke. Going into their top-of-the-table clash with Milan at the end of November, the diminutive Zola had already claimed seven Serie A goals.

But the match failed to live up to the hype. The goalless draw suited Sampdoria as they made it a three-way tie at the top after seeing off Cremonese in Genoa, with Platt and Gullit both on the scoresheet again.

Unlike the previous campaign, we had a genuine title race this time as Milan seemed a shadow of the team they were for the previous two title-winning campaigns. They'd managed just 16 goals over the 13 Serie A games so far – by contrast, at the same stage the previous season, they'd hit the back of the net an astonishing 36 times.

Their forward line had also been weakened further after star winger Gianluigi Lentini was involved in an horrific car crash that nearly cost him his life. He fractured his skull as well as causing considerable damage to an eye socket. It left him in a coma, but thankfully he survived. His career would never reach the same heights, though. He was left with blurred vision at times and eventually he would leave Milan in 1995 with the sad realisation that his best playing days were now behind him.

Weakened up front, it was Milan's defence that was keeping them at the top. With the legendary Dutch trio having left, the champagne football from previous years had been replaced by a reliance on clean sheets. But with a back four of Mauro Tassotti, Franco Baresi, Alessandro Costacurta and Paolo Maldini, they were never likely to concede many.

Over in Turin, Juventus were struggling despite the heroics of club captain Roberto Baggio. The newly crowned Footballer of the Year was on target six times in as many games as he was seemingly on a one-man mission to keep his club's title dreams on track. As the season reached the halfway mark Giovanni Trapattoni's side were three points off the lead along with Sampdoria.

Lazio were in fifth place at the midway point and after having fitness issues early on Gazza was having a better time of it around the turn of the year. It all started against Juventus when his late goal put the seal on a 3–1 win, but things would get better still on a personal level in the New Year. A man of the match performance against Cremonese inspired the Roman side to a 4–2 win at the Stadio

Olimpico. Lazio – and Gazza – would win five out of six league matches. He struck a quite sumptuous free kick in the rout of Cagliari and the following week he would re-enact it for the *Gazzetta* viewers. Gazza – being Gazza – he went the extra mile to include a toy dinosaur (complete with sound effects) as if to replicate coach Dino Zoff.

He was by now producing arguably his finest performances in a Lazio jersey and it would culminate in a glorious night for the club in the Rome derby. Sadly, that didn't involve their British star. He would depart the scene midway through the first half following a crude challenge by Valter Bonacina. Lazio would claim their first derby win in 11 meetings but for their English midfielder, it was seemingly the same story, one of heartbreak as he was about to hit rock-bottom.

In April, his world would fall apart again. A seemingly innocuous training ground challenge on the future Lazio captain – defender Alessandro Nesta – resulted in another broken leg and many felt that'd be the end of the Englishman's Italian adventure. He would return after almost a year out but his second season at the club was over and it wouldn't be all that long before he called time on his Lazio career.

Lazio were without Gazza but they went from strength to strength, losing just one more game. Beppe Signori would finish as Serie A top scorer once again and achieved a feat of his own against Atalanta in mid-April by scoring a hat trick in Lazio's 3–1 win – all of his goals coming from free kicks!

Signori made himself a household name in Italy with his sheer variety of goals. As well as being a clinical free-kick taker, he also had a unique one-step penalty routine, while some of his goals from open play came from his explosive left foot. Even though his feet were only size 5, he became renowned for scoring some memorable goals. All this despite the fact that his right foot was only really needed for standing! He went on to finish as Serie A top scorer in three of his five seasons with Lazio as the Roman club became one of the strongest in the division. Ironically, all this came after being rejected by Inter as a youngster due to his lack of height!

Back in the title race, Milan found themselves two points clear at the top and started the New Year with a trip to Reggiana, a team battling relegation and in their debut season in Italy's top flight. There was nothing remarkable about the game, Marcel Desailly scored shortly before half time and the *rossoneri* ground out another hard-fought win, but it was the start of something truly special, as they would go on another run of clean sheets that would even surpass their remarkable start to the season.

When keeper Sebastiano Rossi was finally beaten – thanks to Igor Kolyvanov's strike for Foggia – it created a new Serie A record of 929 minutes without conceding, beating Dino Zoff's record by 26 minutes, which had been set in 1973. By some strange twist of fate, Kolyvanov was also the man who'd broken Milan's run of clean sheets at the start of the season! It was quite a way for Rossi to mark his first season as the number one goalkeeper for the reigning champions.

Milan went on to win the game 2–1 to now found themselves six points clear of Juventus and Sampdoria at the top. Over the next two weekends Milan effectively sealed the title by seeing off both these sides in what became the new normal in the 1993/94 season – one goal to nil.

Across town the contrast couldn't have been starker as Inter were in deep crisis, leaving coach Osvaldo Bagnoli's job hanging by a thread. His side were seven points behind the leaders and had suffered humiliating defeats – at home to relegation-bound Atalanta and away to struggling Reggiana.

Things came to a head in early February at home to Lazio. The general feeling was that Bagnoli was one defeat away from the sack, but after one of Rubén Sosa's trademark acrobatic strikes it seemed as if Inter were getting back on track. With three minutes remaining, Beppe Signori drew the visitors level and an injury-time strike from Roberto Di Matteo meant it was curtains for Bagnoli. He was replaced by Gianpiero Marini – a scudetto-winner for the club back in 1980.

In the UEFA Cup, it was a completely different story as the club swept to glory, the second time they'd won the trophy in four years. Whether that run affected the club's domestic form we'll never know, but a disastrous end to the season which saw the club gain just nine points from 14 matches meant they would finish just one point above the relegation zone to end the season in 13th place – devastating statistics for a club of Inter's stature. It would be the lowest finish in the club's history.

On the other side of town there was no stopping Milan. Fabio Capello's side had heroes in defence but there was one player who'd effectively seal the title for them during the second half of the campaign. Daniele Massaro had struggled to start matches in previous seasons due to the embarrassment of riches in attack, but he was thrust into the first team by his coach and he'd rewarded Capello handsomely. Massaro struck seven goals in nine games – many of them match-winning strikes, the most memorable of which came in the final moments of the Milan derby.

By the time Milan travelled to Naples in late March they found themselves nine points clear at the top – and with just six games left the title was all but decided. Their opponents in week 29 were reaching the end of a quite remarkable season of their own. Back in the summer they'd appointed a new coach – a certain Marcello Lippi – and he'd made quite an impact. Having made an impression with unfashionable Atalanta a year earlier he headed south to one of the biggest jobs in Italian football.

Beset by financial problems following the golden years of Diego Maradona, Lippi guided his team into the UEFA Cup on the final day of the season. Their most notable result came against the champions-elect in late March. Talismanic forward Paolo Di Canio scored one of the goals of the season ten minutes from time, a stunning solo effort after turning the Milan defence inside out – no mean achievement in itself. It was a first defeat in 19 matches for Capello's men.

They were still seven points clear though – meaning the title race was all but won. A draw with Udinese at the San Siro in mid-April secured a third straight title, but it really had lacked the flair of the previous two. Just 15 goals conceded in 34 matches was the lynchpin of their success as they only scored 36 times themselves; only seven teams had scored fewer in the entire division.

At the bottom, the relegation battle was, as ever, full of drama. With four teams to be relegated two spots remained to join the hapless Lecce and Atalanta in Serie B and they all faced daunting away trips.

Udinese had possibly the toughest of the lot, facing a revitalised Juventus side in Turin, while local rivals – Piacenza and Reggiana – would be travelling to Parma and recently crowned champions Milan respectively, with the *rossoneri* appearing to be going through the motions.

The Parma versus Piacenza derby clash was actually brought forward to the Saturday evening due to Parma's upcoming appointment with Arsenal in the Cup Winners' Cup final. Would this give Luigi Cagni's side an advantage?

The match at the Ennio Tardini stadium finished goalless, meaning Udinese had to win against Juventus to be involved in a play-off for the second consecutive season. Anything else would mean relegation. Reggiana meanwhile were a point behind Piacenza so nothing less than a win for them would do at the San Siro, after Piacenza had edged the clubs' head-to-head meetings during the season.

Udinese would ultimately go down to a 1–0 defeat in Turin courtesy of a Gianluca Vialli goal, but who would be joining them in Serie B? It was an incredibly tense afternoon and at the San Siro the deadlock was broken with 20 minutes left. Massimiliano Esposito struck the goal of his career to put Reggiana ahead. With Milan offering precious little in attack it would prove enough as Piacenza were relegated, which was understandably hard to take.

The *rossoneri* did have a huge clash ahead of them in the European Cup Final against Barcelona but their passive performance on the final day of the season was less than impressive. They were a shadow of the side that had just won the title, so Piacenza had plenty to feel aggrieved about.

In truth though, that final-day loss summed up Milan's poor end-of-season performances, as in the end they won the title by just three points. Just like 12 months earlier, they limped over the line after failing to win any of their last six matches.

In the meantime, Juventus had slipped under the radar, losing just one game since mid-December, meaning they finished runners-up. But unlike Milan they'd been playing with flair. Gianluca Vialli was finally back – and scoring goals for fun. He would claim four in the last three games to serve notice of what lay ahead in the next 12 months.

They'd also introduced a young forward to the first team by the name of Alessandro Del Piero. On his full first-team debut he made quite an impact – netting a hat-trick against Parma.

A 6–1 demolition of Lazio in mid-April featuring a Vialli hat-trick and a goal of the season contender from Roberto Baggio secured the club's biggest win of the season. For the first time in the past few years Milan's era of domination was looking under serious threat. This Juventus side was beginning to look the real deal, even without inspirational captain Roberto Baggio. He'd been frustrated by injury problems during the second half of the season but his absence from the side had made little difference. A wind of change was blowing through Italian football.

3

THE MAGIC OF MARCELLO

The Juventus hierarchy knew they couldn't stand still. They'd gained so much momentum during the final weeks of the 1993/94 season that this was the moment to build on that and they didn't see coach Giovanni Trapattoni as the man to deliver a first scudetto in almost a decade. So, the veteran left for Bayern Munich and they found what they hoped would be the perfect replacement.

Marcello Lippi had performed miracles over the past couple of seasons, guiding unfashionable Atalanta to seventh in 1993 and following that by achieving UEFA Cup qualification with Napoli 12 months later. He'd done all of this without the financial backing he'd have liked, but Juventus had taken notice and been impressed. The exciting brand of football his teams played further enhanced his CV – he was appointed Juventus coach in the summer of 1994 with one target: win the scudetto.

There were big changes in the boardroom too as President Umberto Agnelli created the famous (or perhaps infamous as time would prove) "Triade" of directors to oversee all football operations. Legendary striker Roberto Bettega was appointed Vice President of the club and would be joined by Antonio Giraudo as the new CEO and Luciano Moggi as Sporting Director.

This was a revitalised Juventus and over the summer the new coach had been busy assembling a squad capable of ending their long wait for the scudetto – they hadn't been champions of Italy in almost a decade.

Lippi put together a fantastic squad. Angelo Peruzzi had made the goalkeeping position his own but the defence was bolstered by the arrival of Ciro Ferrara. Lippi was well aware of his versatility. He could play at right back as well as his more natural role in the centre of defence.

The midfield was bolstered by the arrival of former European Cup winner Didier Deschamps. He was joined by Portuguese international Paulo Sousa, who arrived from Sporting Lisbon. The attack didn't need any additions. Gianluca Vialli, Fabrizio Ravanelli, Roberto Baggio and Alessandro Del Piero were already four of the hottest properties in European football.

Lippi though didn't want his new-look Juventus to be as dependent on Baggio as they had been in previous seasons. He needed more goals from Ravanelli and Vialli. They'd struck just 24 times between them in the previous couple of seasons; that simply wasn't enough if the team were to have a realistic shot at the title. They also had Alessandro Del Piero. After breaking through at the end of the previous season, great things were expected of him – and the 1994/95 season would mark his coming of age.

Before a ball was kicked in anger though, plenty had changed in Serie A. The Italian Football Federation had made the decision to finally join the rest of European football by awarding three points for a win. There were plenty of changes around the division, and for me personally too.

After a year as runner I'd now been promoted to working in our VT department. This role would require me to record two links from James Richardson in the stadium and edit them with the two pre-match VTs that had been cut the previous Friday to make one pre-recorded package at the top of the show for us to play out, lasting between four to five minutes. Sound simple? Some weeks it was, but sometimes the links came rather too close to on-air for comfort, so we had more than a few hairy moments over the years.

Back on the field, Fiorentina were back in Serie A after storming to the second division title. They'd be joined in the top flight by Brescia – who just like the *viola* had been relegated the year before. Bari were back for the first time since the days of David Platt and

Padova would be gracing the top flight for the first time in 32 years. It had been a busy summer in the transfer market too as Juventus had not been the only club spending money.

The biggest changes were in the capital. At Roma both Jonas Thern and Daniel Fonseca had been signed from Napoli – and the latter would create a lethal South American attacking partnership with Abel Balbo. The pair would go on to score 30 times between them during the course of the 1994/95 campaign.

Across town at Lazio there was a change on the bench as Dino Zoff was replaced by the more attack-minded Zdeněk Zeman. The Czech had performed miracles with unfashionable Foggia and would once again be linking up with Beppe Signori, Serie A's top scorer for the past two seasons. With Alen Bokšić and Pierluigi Casiraghi to call on too, Zeman would have an embarrassment of riches up front and unsurprisingly they'd turn out to be the league's highest scorers.

It had also been a summer of change in the northern city of Genoa. Gianluca Pagliuca, who'd just added a second Coppa Italia to the title he'd won at Sampdoria in 1991, switched to Inter for £6.5 million with the hugely experienced Walter Zenga moving in the opposite direction.

The big news coming from the port city revolved around a certain Dutchman. Ruud Gullit – who'd made the switch to the Marassi stadium from Milan 12 months earlier – stunned everyone by returning to the San Siro. After scoring 15 times for Sven-Göran Eriksson's side – including the goal which beat Milan in one of the games of the season – he was reunited with Fabio Capello.

Sampdoria's rivals Genoa were also busy and made history, snapping up Kazu Miura on loan from Japanese side Verdy Kawasaki, in the process becoming the first Japanese player to ply his trade in Serie A. He would make a name for himself in Italian football by scoring in the "*derby della lanterna*" (derby of the lighthouse).

Going into the new season there was plenty of talk about two attacking players who would not only go on to win titles but become captains and symbols of their clubs – Alessandro Del Piero of Juventus and Francesco Totti of Roma.

After joining from Padova in the summer of 1993 and subsequently breaking through to the first team, great things were now expected of the Juventus youngster. The hat-trick towards the end of the 1993/94 season against Parma had only added to the fans' expectations.

Some 700 kilometres further south, people were now starting to talk of Francesco Totti. Roman born and bred and a former ball boy at the Stadio Olimpico, he'd broken into the first team and featured in the Rome derby back in March – winning the penalty that should have drawn his side level. The player who missed that spot kick was Giuseppe Giannini and Totti was very much seen as his heir apparent. The similarities were endless: both local lads, both huge fans of the club, and both would wear the number 10 jersey for Roma with distinction.

Del Piero and Totti would be in their respective teams' starting XIs as Serie A kicked off in early September. Francesco Totti struck his first Roma goal at home to Foggia although in the end the *giallorossi* would have to settle for a 1–1 draw.

Del Piero meanwhile was also in the starting line-up as Juventus began life under Lippi with a trip to newly promoted Brescia, and just like Roma they were held to a disappointing draw and found themselves behind Milan already. They needn't have panicked though. Despite kicking off with a win over Genoa, the *rossoneri*'s title defence was about to get off to a disastrous start.

After opening up at home with a routine win over Bari in front of the *Football Italia* cameras, Juventus were off and underway. The following week saw them make the long trip south to Naples on what was an emotional night for coach Lippi and native Neapolitan Ciro Ferrara, returning home after just a few months. As for the game, Juventus served notice of their intent. Goals from Fabrizio Ravanelli and a stunner from the much-hyped Alessandro Del Piero maintained the unbeaten start.

There were some other stories beginning to develop in the season's opening weeks. Roma had also got off to a flier thanks in no small part to their attack. The Balbo–Fonseca partnership had the rest of Serie A sitting up and taking notice – they'd struck ten times in the first seven games to lead Roma to the top of the standings.

But things weren't going so well for the two Milanese clubs. Inter found themselves well off the pace by the end of October after suffering a home defeat to Serie A new boys Bari. Milan had also endured a terrible start to their title defence and the defeat to another newly promoted side – Padova – followed a defeat at Cremonese. It wasn't just the results that were poor but the performances too. Those losses had raised plenty of questions for fans and media alike. Was it the end of the road for this great Milan side? It was the first time Fabio Capello's men had been under pressure in several years as they found themselves five points off the pace already. But with three points for a win now having been introduced in Italy, this was a far from insurmountable deficit to make up.

In late October, they travelled to Juventus for a fixture they dared not lose. Two defeats in three had left them well off the pace. Not that things were all that rosy for the *bianconeri* as Juventus themselves had suffered a slight wobble. Defeat in Foggia meant they were now two points behind pace-setters Parma – and that defeat led to some in-house recriminations, with President Umberto Agnelli far from impressed.

For the third straight season just one goal settled the latest Juventus versus Milan clash, but this time it came from Juventus, as Roberto Baggio headed home from Angelo Di Livio's cross. It was a huge moment in the *bianconeri*'s season but it wasn't just the defeat that would have alarmed Milan. They barely forced Angelo Peruzzi into a save during the whole 90 minutes as their fall from grace got worse by the week.

Juventus though would soon be playing catch-up. Their next fixture was the derby with Torino but it had to be postponed after days of torrential rain in Italy's north-west. On the same day as the scheduled Turin derby, 150 kilometres away at the San Siro our match on Channel 4 was Milan versus Parma, which was played in monsoon-like conditions. The match ended in a draw as Milan's struggles showed no signs of abating.

The power shift looked to be tilting towards Turin. Even though they were a point behind Parma, Juventus were starting to believe that this could be a special season. Wins over Reggiana and Padova followed ahead of Fiorentina's visit to the Stadio delle Alpi. This match had been billed as a massive test not only of Fiorentina's resurgence but also of Juve's title credentials.

After storming to the Serie B title and making their stay outside Italy's top flight as brief a one as possible, Claudio Ranieri's side had made a stunning return to Serie A. By the end of November they were third, just a point behind Juventus and a further point back from leaders Parma. They'd lost just once, were scoring for fun and had created history.

Star striker Gabriel Batistuta had struck in all of the club's first 11 league games – breaking a record set by Ezio Pascutti of Bologna some 30 years earlier. But their recent record in this fixture hadn't been good, with just one league win away to Juventus in 20 years.

They started this match in stunning fashion. First-half goals from Francesco Baiano and Angelo Carbone had them in dreamland at the break. Juventus didn't know what had hit them.

The home side struggled to make any sort of impact. Fiorentina were cruising and seemingly on their way to a famous win, before Juventus finally woke up. With just over a quarter of an hour remaining, Gianluca Vialli's bullet header halved the deficit and incredibly a couple of minutes later it was all square thanks to that man Vialli once again, as he pounced on a loose ball inside the box and placed his shot past Francesco Toldo.

The match had been turned on its head and suddenly it was all Juventus, they had Fiorentina pinned back but the visitors had seemingly ridden out the storm. Enter Alessandro Del Piero. With just a couple of minutes remaining he made it 3–2 with an outrageous volley to send the home fans into raptures.

The goal would be one of the iconic moments of the season. Del Piero had come into the side after captain Roberto Baggio had sustained a serious knee injury at Padova just seven days earlier. Another week on and Del Piero was at it again, scoring another contender for goal of the season as Juventus edged a seven-goal thriller against Lazio.

Elsewhere the *Football Italia* cameras had been present at the Stadio Olimpico for the first of the two capital-city derbies with Roma desperate to avenge their defeat to Lazio back in March – and what a show they put on! Goals from Balbo, Cappioli and Fonseca gained ample revenge as Roma earned a first win over Lazio in two and a half years.

Things were finally beginning to pick up for Milan. Their start to the season had left them with no chance of winning the scudetto but 11 unbeaten games either side of the New Year restored some respectability to a season which had in truth never got started.

There was little cheer at Inter though. Defeat to relegation-threatened Padova left them in the bottom half of the table. A squad which boasted the likes of Uruguayan star Rubén Sosa, Dutch duo Dennis Bergkamp and Wim Jonk, Italian international keeper Gianluca Pagliuca as well as club legend Giuseppe Bergomi was struggling. Just two wins in nine games had left the club 15 points behind leaders Juventus.

It wasn't just in the league that the season had been a disappointment though. Out of Europe in the UEFA Cup second round as well as going out of the Coppa Italia in the quarter finals had left the club with very little to play for. Qualifying for Europe remained the sole objective and even that looked a tall order. At the half way point of the season Inter were languishing just four points above the relegation zone. Despite the UEFA Cup win in May, 1994 had been a disastrous year for the club.

By contrast Juventus were flying and 1995 kicked off with the game of the season as they faced Parma in a top-of-the-table clash at the Ennio Tardini stadium. It would prove to be one of the pivotal matches of the season. Despite going a goal down early in the second half, Marcello Lippi's side would storm back to win 3–1 thanks in no small part to Fabrizio Ravanelli's header – one of the goals of the season.

So, Juventus were top – and they'd stay there for the rest of the season even if the steam train hit the buffers in quite spectacular fashion in January as they suffered back-to-back defeats, conceding six goals in the process. First, they went down to a shock 3–0 defeat at Cagliari but what followed was even more surprising as Torino edged a five-goal thriller in a breathless *"Derby della Mole"*. Fabrizio Ravanelli's missed penalty condemned Juve to defeat.

But on 29 January 1995 football in Italy was a mere afterthought. *Football Italia* was on air for the Genoa versus Milan match live from the Stadio Luigi Ferraris. After a scoreless first half James Richardson was analysing the action with studio guest Luther Blissett and before long there seemed an unnatural anger on the terraces. Soon fighting was breaking out, the police were firing water cannon and in those very early days of the internet the lack of information was a real problem in what was an increasingly tense atmosphere.

With the violence intensifying in the stands, the decision was taken by the referee to abandon the match. Meanwhile, outside the stadium, a full-scale riot was taking place. Cars were being smashed, police were trying to quell the unrest with more water cannons and the injured were being escorted to hospital.

All of this was the result of the fatal stabbing of young Genoa fan Vincenzo Spagnolo outside the ground prior to kick-off following tensions between rival supporters. After word had reached the Genoa ultras of Spagnolo's death, the home fans were determined to have the match abandoned and were prepared to do anything to achieve this.

Shockwaves reverberated around Serie A. The following week, fixtures were postponed as the nation reflected on the shocking events in Genoa. The Italian Football Federation called for a "week of reflection". Such was the tension between the two clubs that they imposed a ban on away supporters when they faced one another that was only brought to an end in 2010.

Genoa paid their own respects to Vincenzo and in the years that followed the club set up a pre-season friendly tournament in his honour – the Trofeo Spagnolo.

A fortnight after the tragedy, Serie A resumed with a message from both captains prior to kick-off in all the matches, pleading for an end to football violence. Despite an horrific fortnight for *calcio* the focus was back on the beautiful game and there were some lovely stories developing during the 1994/95 season.

One of them was Bari. They were hosting leaders Juventus at the San Nicola stadium and had been the season's surprise package. Following their last Serie A experience, which ended in relegation in 1992, coach Giuseppe Materazzi had put together a squad that was performing way above expectations. Sandro Tovalieri had already struck 12 times as his side picked up some unexpected results, winning away to Lazio, Inter and Milan.

Tovalieri had scored crucial goals in all of those matches and although it was relatively late in his career he'd finally made his mark in Italy's top flight. The visit of Juventus to the San Nicola stadium would prove too much for him and his side though. Goals from Alessandro Del Piero and a rare strike from Ciro Ferrara ensured yet another win for the league leaders as they maintained their three-point lead at the top.

That advantage would become six the following week. While Juventus were earning a narrow win over Napoli, it was a very different story in Sardinia where Parma went down 2–0 at Cagliari, who were making a habit of upsetting the top sides. Roma, in fact, were the only team in the top six to come away from Sardinia with a victory.

But it wasn't just Parma who were having a bad week. Milan's 11-match unbeaten run in Serie A came to a shuddering halt as they were thrashed 4–0 by Lazio, a side who would score goals for fun in the early months of 1995. As well as the mauling of Milan they beat Genoa by the same scoreline and would go on to beat relegation-bound Foggia 7–1. Amazingly, the side from the capital would soon surpass that with an astonishing 8–2 rout of Fiorentina.

In the meantime, there was also encouraging news off the field as Gazza was closing in on a return to action following his long recovery from the horrific broken leg he'd suffered some 12 months earlier.

That return came in early April against ideal opposition. Reggiana were a team heading for relegation. After dramatically staying up on the final day of the previous campaign, the 1994/95 season would prove to be a disastrous one for the club. They would gain just one point on the road all season and finish a staggering 22 points from safety.

One of their 24 defeats came at Lazio on what was a very special day, as Gazza made his long-awaited comeback. After a year on the sidelines, the Geordie star was back under a different coach, the chain-smoking Czech Zdeněk Zeman.

Zeman was a veteran of the Italian game. Despite never playing at a professional level he became a coach and went on to manage a total of 11 past and present Serie A clubs, including spells with both Lazio and Roma as well as Napoli.

But he made his name at Foggia during his second spell at the club between 1989 and 1994. After being appointed to what was then a Serie C (third division) club, he led them to back-to-back promotions, in the process unearthing some Serie A stars of the future. His famous attacking 4–3–3 formation brought the best out of them and the three forwards would move on to some of the biggest clubs in the country.

Beppe Signori would become a team mate of Gazza's at Lazio and a hugely successful career would culminate in him scoring 188 Serie A goals in his career. While his team mates up front wouldn't boast the same numbers in terms of goals they went on to achieve great things. The second member of the trio was Francesco Baiano. He would spend much of his career with Fiorentina – partnering the legendary Gabriel Batistuta up front. Like the Argentine, Baiano would stay loyal to the *viola* despite relegation from Serie A in 1993 and would be a key part of Fiorentina's success in the mid-'90s, winning both the Italian Cup and Super Cup in 1996. Finally, Roberto Rambaudi would link up with Zeman again at Lazio in 1994 and during his successful spell in the capital would earn two caps for the national team. He played alongside Gazza for a couple of months at the end of the 1994/95 season as the British midfielder made his return.

Gazza's reintroduction to the starting line-up coincided with a good run of form for Lazio, as they saw off some of the biggest names in Serie A – and in some style too. A 2–0 win derby win over Roma was followed by big wins against Juventus and Inter as Zeman's side finished the season impressively.

That defeat for the champions-elect made it three consecutive defeats at the Stadio delle Alpi. After winning away to Milan at the start of April and going nine points clear at the top, they then lost the derby once again to earn Torino, their bitter rivals, a league double over Juventus for the first time in almost half a century.

A fortnight later Padova secured the shock result of the season, winning 1–0 in Turin and that was followed by the *bianconeri*'s heaviest loss of the season against Lazio. The Roman club recorded a staggering 3–0 win in Turin thanks to three goals in the last 20 minutes in a game which Juventus had completely dominated.

Juventus were winning away from home, however, scoring four times at both Fiorentina and Genoa. Just prior to that Fiorentina match though – and four months since the tragic loss of Vincenzo Spagnolo – Italian football was once again left in mourning, following the tragic death of young Andrea Fortunato.

The hugely popular left-back hadn't featured at all during the season after being diagnosed with leukaemia, but, after seemingly recovering, he caught pneumonia from which he never recovered. It left Juventus – and the whole country – completely shattered. Club captain Gianluca Vialli broke down in tears at the funeral in Fortunato's home town of Salerno, before paying tribute to his team mate:

> Dear Andrea,
> We will forever hold you in our hearts. We remember you with happiness for what we achieved together, even though it was painfully short. We hope that there is a football team in heaven so you can continue to be happy running with the ball at your feet. Honour to you my brother.

Devastated off the pitch, glory – and a first league title in nine years – awaited Juventus on it. The gap to second-placed Parma was now seven points and with three games to play the two would meet in Turin.

It would be the first in a series of clashes between Italy's top two over the final month of the season. They would meet in the UEFA Cup Final, where Parma would be victorious, adding another European trophy to their collection. (They'd already won the Cup Winners' Cup at Wembley two years earlier.) It would be a different story in the final of the Coppa Italia though, with Juventus cruising to a 3–0 aggregate victory.

But for both these clubs it was all about Serie A. Juventus had been top since the turn of the year and were so close to a long-overdue title. Parma were the *nouveaux riches* of the Italian game thanks to the financial muscle of global giants Parmalat who were bankrolling the club, but despite success at home and abroad had yet to taste glory in Serie A.

And on a warm early summer afternoon in Turin, Juventus knew that a draw would be enough to seal the title. Despite not needing a victory, they were desperate to seal the scudetto with a win and a performance that would characterise the campaign they'd had.

This new-look Juventus under Marcello Lippi was a world away from the team that had struggled to put together a title challenge in recent years. They were on the brink and the packed out Stadio delle Alpi – which was something of a rarity in itself – was expectant.

Two goals from Ravanelli, one for Vialli and a delightful move finished off by Didier Deschamps saw Juventus crowned champions as Parma were well and truly put to the sword.

As referee Piero Ceccarini blew his final whistle it was party time in Turin as thousands of fans invaded the pitch, desperate to get hold of their heroes. In the end Juventus would win the title by a massive ten points. Marcello Lippi in his debut season in Turin had won a scudetto for the *bianconeri* – and in glorious fashion. Quite appropriately, the triumph was dedicated to the late Andrea Fortunato.

So, what had made the difference from previous seasons? How had Juventus gone from also-rans to the top of the Italian game in 12 months? The answer lay up front. The attacking pair of Gianluca Vialli and Fabrizio Ravanelli – who'd struggled in previous seasons – amassed 32 goals between them in Serie A.

While the club had to live without club captain Roberto Baggio for much of the campaign it had also been a real breakthrough year for youngster Alessandro Del Piero. Lippi's intention from the outset had been to make the side less reliant on Baggio than in previous seasons and in Del Piero he'd found the perfect replacement.

The 21-year-old started at Padova before Juventus began showing interest in him. He was signed for just over £2 million and before long was knocking on the door of the first team. A hat-trick against Parma in the spring of 1994 introduced him to the world stage before he really came of age under Marcello Lippi.

After the dust had settled on the Juventus title triumph there was plenty happening behind the scenes in Turin. The club's hierarchy came to the conclusion that Del Piero was the club's future and offered Baggio an extension to his contract, but only at 50% of his current salary. Del Piero would go on to take Baggio's famous number ten shirt ahead of the 1995/96 season.

Suddenly clubs at home and abroad were interested and Baggio was sold to Milan for £6.8 million amid protests from the Juventus supporters. This transfer would be a sign of times to come – the *bianconeri* top brass would sell stars but recruit in such a way that the club would still be highly competitive on the field. Gianluca Vialli in 1996, Christian Vieri in 1997 and the biggest of all – Zinedine Zidane in 2001. They would all be examples of the big Juventus summer sales during their glory years, but it didn't seem to matter. The season after each of those had left would see Juventus crowned champions.

Vialli would be replaced by Christian Vieri, who a year later would be replaced by Filippo Inzaghi. Zidane seemed irreplaceable but in the summer of 2001 in came the hugely impressive Pavel Nedvěd from Lazio, who would go on to win scudetti with the club in his first two seasons in Turin. Big names leaving, big names signing. Big titles being won.

In the short-term though, the whole of Italian football was asking the same question. Had Juventus' decision to sell Baggio given Milan a big advantage ahead of the new season?

After finishing fourth, Fabio Capello's men would be desperate to regain the title. And this was a new-look Milan. They were raring to go and fight to win back the scudetto. Had Juventus just handed them back the initiative?

4

ROARING LIONS

While it had been celebration time in Turin it was an emotional summer in London as it was the end of an era. Both Paul Gascoigne and David Platt were waving farewell to Italy – both departing prior to the 1995/96, our fourth season of coverage.

Gazza's three years in Italy had been an emotional rollercoaster. They'd featured him fighting back from injuries, being the unwanted centre of attention off the field as well as showing occasional flashes of the brilliance Lazio had been expecting following his multi-million-pound transfer from Tottenham.

There had been highlights, like the last-gasp equaliser in the Rome derby which triggered a fantastic run of form. More injuries blighted him during the second half of 1993, although before that he produced arguably his finest performances for the Roman club either side of the New Year.

He was a regular starter and was scoring some fantastic goals as Lazio embarked on a run of just three defeats in 19 Serie A games, thanks in no small part to their English star. Arguably the highlight of that run was the long-overdue derby win over Roma after five barren years. Unfortunately, Gazza would be forced to go off in that game and his world would be turned upside down just a month later after he broke his leg during a training session.

When he finally returned to action, he soon became frustrated over coach Zdeněk Zeman's strict regime (not to mention being regularly played out of position) and the Geordie star called it quits in the capital. When Rangers offered Lazio a club record fee of £4.3 million to acquire his services it marked the end of his Italian adventure and he was off to Glasgow.

Gazza had been incredibly popular with the fans as well as his team mates during his time in Serie A – and it wasn't just the Italian media and fans who'd grown to love him. He'd made a huge impact on *Gazzetta Football Italia* too. By now the show had a big following in the UK as he pulled off all manner of pranks during his time in the Italian capital. The viewers would see him let the tyres down of team mate Aron Winter's Ferrari, take coach Zdeněk Zeman's whistle and tie it around a goose and position an enormous ray fish on the windscreen of star striker Beppe Signori. For English viewers, it wasn't just the football they tuned in for – Gazza's pranks were all part of the fun.

Many football fans weren't prepared to fork out hard-earned cash for a Sky subscription and in those early years of the Premier League, Serie A was the best league in Europe – boasting a vast array of domestic and foreign talent. These *stranieri* – or overseas players – were drawn to the big clubs in Italy who in the 1990s dominated the game on a global scale.

Not only that but Channel 4's coverage was the only place where lovers of the beautiful game could enjoy live football every week on terrestrial television – and there were millions tuning in.

Italy's other British import – David Platt – was about to say goodbye too. After four years abroad – the last two of which being hugely successful with Sampdoria – the temptation of signing for Arsenal was just too good to turn down as he headed for home.

Football Italia viewers needn't have worried though, as we had a replacement lined up. Paul Ince touched down in Italy during the summer of 1995. After a trophy-laden six years at Manchester United the self-styled "Guvnor" joined Inter Milan for £7.5 million.

But just like with Gazza, the English international would have a hard job in Italy. With very few players at the club speaking English, he not only had to learn a new language but also help awaken a sleeping giant of Serie A. Inter had won the title just once in over 15 years and despite UEFA Cup success in 1994, the past 18 months had been little short of disastrous for one of the biggest and most illustrious clubs in Italy. The acquisition of not only Ince but also future club legend Javier Zanetti and the explosive Brazilian Roberto Carlos from Real Madrid promised better things.

Inter had a reputation for signing top talent from Europe. The late 1980s had seen them snap up the German trio of Lothar Matthäus, defender Andreas Brehme and prolific striker Jürgen Klinsmann – all of whom were integral parts of Germany's World Cup-winning team in 1990.

Their city rivals Milan had of course enjoyed the services of a special trio of their own – Netherlands internationals Ruud Gullit, Marco van Basten and Frank Rijkaard – who would go on to domestic and European glory with the club.

And it wasn't just in Milan that Italian clubs were shopping abroad. Juventus had snapped up another German duo in the shape of Jürgen Kohler and Andreas Möller. Roma and Lazio had both scoured the Bundesliga for talent too, in the shape of Karl-Heinz Riedle, Thomas Doll and Thomas Häessler.

There was also a very strong South American presence now plying its trade in Italy's top flight. Whether it was the warm climate, the similarity in language or the success of the Italian clubs in Europe, it was the place to play for the cream of the South American crop.

During the course of the 1990s all of Serie A's top clubs would boast a South American influence, led by Inter Milan. Uruguayans Rubén Sosa and Álvaro Recoba, Chile's Iván Zamorano. Long-serving stalwart Javier Zanetti as well as Brazilian World Cup-winner Roberto Carlos would all have successful careers with the *nerazzurri*. But one man would make a bigger impact than anyone else at the club. After a much-protracted transfer from Barcelona, Ronaldo would become a goalscoring sensation at the San Siro, as Inter became a huge force both domestically and in Europe.

It was further south though that the South American influence would kick off. After Diego Maradona had inspired Napoli to their first league title in 1987 the floodgates were opened for an influx of *stranieri*. In came Brazilian Careca and Uruguayan Daniel Fonseca, who would eventually strike up a lethal partnership in Naples.

Fiorentina though signed the South American player who would arguably have the most impact in the club's history and one of the greatest imports of all – Gabriel Batistuta. Having broken goalscoring records as well as staying loyal to the club following relegation in 1993 he was the iconic figure of the club in the '90s – revered so much that the fans built a statue of him which in the 1990s had pride of place by the pitch at the Stadio Artemio Franchi.

The one team to have less of a South American influence was AC Milan. Ahead of the 1995/96 season the *rossoneri* had strengthened significantly with the transfer of Roberto Baggio from Juventus. As well as the former World Player of the Year, Fabio Capello had identified another man who would be key. The club paid Paris Saint-Germain £6 million for Liberian striker George Weah. It would turn out to be a master stroke of a signing. In his first year at the club he would join Baggio in winning that illustrious world-topping honour.

Fabio Capello and his men had a ruthless determination about them. Their mission: to win the Serie A title back from a Juventus side that had swept all before them over the previous twelve months. With Baggio and Weah in their squad, they had every chance of doing so.

There was huge anticipation ahead of the 1995/96 season as the new Serie A took shape. Gone were Brescia, Reggiana, Foggia and Genoa – who'd lost a heartbreaking play-off defeat to Padova on penalties. Genoa's relegation in particular was desperately sad and it robbed viewers of two classic derby matches with Sampdoria. The most recent of those was a memorable one for all of us working on *Football Italia* as Elvis Costello was our guest in the stadium, and in one of the most entertaining few minutes on air, James Richardson had guided us through the half-time scores with as many references to his songs as possible!

Vicenza – champions of Serie B – were among the Serie A new boys to replace Genoa et al, and there were three other teams who were making an immediate return to Italy's top flight – Piacenza, Udinese and Atalanta. All four would avoid relegation and all four of them would make headlines.

Vicenza were back in Serie A for the first time in 20 years and it'd prove to be just the start of a golden period in their history. The club that brought through the legendary Paolo Rossi would soon be causing shockwaves around Italy. Under Francesco Guidolin they would stun all of Serie A's biggest names by winning the Coppa Italia and subsequently making it to the semi-finals of the Cup Winners' Cup.

Fellow Serie A new boys Udinese had appointed a coach by the name of Alberto Zaccheroni. Both he and the club would go on to great success – the club became regular qualifiers for European competition and within four years Zaccheroni would be landing the coaching job with Milan.

Despite being relative novices in European competition, the club had acquired a reputation for attracting some of South America's finest talent. Before the capture of Argentinian Abel Balbo from River Plate, they had also snapped up Brazilian World Cup-winner Zico, who proved to be a revelation in his first season with the club. He finished second in the goalscoring charts, becoming a renowned set-piece specialist.

Piacenza were champions of Serie B in 1995 and despite being back in the big time the club would create a policy of having an all-Italian playing roster. This gained many admirers up and down the country; in these heady days of Serie A being awash with money and the cream of the world's talent, this was a small, provincial club doing it their way – and succeeding.

At the top, the summer of 1995 had seen all manner of changes around Italy's top flight. While Milan had signed Weah and Baggio, across town at Inter there was a veritable revolution taking place. Oil magnate Massimo Moratti had taken over the club and in his first transfer window as President wasn't afraid to splash the cash. As well as the purchase of England's Paul Ince and Roberto Carlos they also snapped up two of Serie A's more underrated forwards – the hugely talented Benito Carbone from Napoli and prolific striker Maurizio Ganz, who'd just enjoyed three successful years with Atalanta. The only constant was the club retaining Ottavio Bianchi as coach. After a mediocre first season, many remained unconvinced.

Juventus had been busy too and completed a triple swoop from Sampdoria. In came midfielder Vladimir Jugović, central defender Pietro Vierchowod and flying winger Attilio Lombardo.

Sampdoria needed reinforcements and went shopping at home and abroad. In came striker Enrico Chiesa from Cremonese. The 24-year-old had struck 14 times in what was a struggling side so Sven-Göran Eriksson saw plenty of promise in him, which would turn out to prove more than justified. 22 goals later, he forced his way into the Italy squad for the European Championships. The Sampdoria coach also added two overseas internationals: in came Clarence Seedorf from European champions Ajax and Christian Karembeu from Nantes.

Torino had also been busy as they signed Turkish striker Hakan Şükür from Galatasaray. However, his short stay in Italy would be a fairly disastrous one. It lasted six months, during which time he featured for the club five times, scoring just the one goal.

Down in the capital there was mutiny on the streets. The Lazio President Sergio Cragnotti had accepted a £22 million bid from Parma for the services of star striker Beppe Signori and the club was willing to sell. Hundreds of ultras lined the streets to express their anger, hurling coins and tomatoes at the club's headquarters. The proposed transfer was scrapped.

No Signori to Parma then, but the Emilian club were still busy in the transfer market, signing Hristo Stoichkov from Barcelona as well as Fabio Cannavaro from Napoli.

And on to the much-hyped start to the season, and while the league had seen numerous changes in personnel over the summer months, *Gazzetta Football Italia* had a newcomer of its own. My boss thought it might be a good idea to have a new voice on the goals round up as we used Gary Bloom on commentary edits on Serie A, Coppa Italia and European match highlights for the show.

The production hierarchy thought it might be a good idea to have an Italian voice on the programme so in stepped Luigi V.R. Chiappini, who would do the goals round up on a Thursday afternoon. He'd arrive on his bicycle, read through the scripts, drink his coffee and off we'd go! Luigi had no sports background, and while the idea to use him seemed like a good one, in reality it didn't work as well as well as we'd hoped (through no fault of Luigi's) as he wasn't so comfortable with the names of the players. Indeed, towards the end of what was his only season on the production, I was talked into doing a mock voiceover, impersonating him on one of the goals round-up matches and my mischievous editor would then insert it into the programme the following day. Needless to say, my boss noticed and soon realised I'd been up to no good in between fits of laughter. The following summer it was decided that Kenneth Wolstenholme would revoice the goals round-up – to put it simply, the Luigi V.R. Chiappini experiment was an imaginative idea but was to be sadly curtailed.

Back on the field, Milan were desperate to get their title back, and they looked to be on a mission from day one. An opening-round win over Padova featured a debut goal for Weah and the rarity of a Franco Baresi winner, but this was just the start. The *rossoneri* won their first four games with Weah and Baggio among the goals – they actually supplied over half of the club's nine goals during the opening month of the campaign. But the first setback was just around the corner.

Defeat at Bari proved to be no more of a blip, but at the time it seemed far more serious as star signing Roberto Baggio limped off. Despite his absence Milan went from strength to strength. Just seven days after that defeat in Bari, Milan faced their biggest test of the season so far, as Juventus were the visitors. Just six months earlier the champions-elect had cruised to a 2–0 victory at the San Siro on what was a pivotal night on their march to the scudetto.

But this was a different Milan. The *rossoneri* raced into a 2–0 lead after just a quarter of an hour thanks to goals from Marco Simone and the ever-impressive George Weah. His decisive strike inflicted a first defeat of the season on the champions and despite a late consolation from Alessandro Del Piero, Juventus were unable to force an equaliser. It was a sign of things to come.

Parma were doing their best to keep up with the league leaders but their star man was having a mixed time of it. The signing of Hristo Stoichkov was a statement of intent from the club, having failed to land Signori, and despite starting well things would soon start to go wrong both on the field and off it.

The Bulgarian forward was getting increasingly frustrated by the team selection and choices of coach Nevio Scala, but that was just the tip of the iceberg. He became increasingly irritable with Italian referees as well as the media. His reluctance to speak to the Italian press did nothing for his popularity, which sunk even lower as Spanish daily newspaper *Marca* got all of his attention. Whether it was a trust issue or a language barrier was pretty unclear but with Stoichkov's Barcelona past, it didn't sit well with the club or their supporters. His time in Italy lasted all of one season, during which his off-field histrionics did him no favours and a young star by the name of Filippo Inzaghi would feature more and more in his place.

Initially, things had started well in Italy for Stoichkov. He'd struck four goals by the start of October and before too long Parma had joined Fabio Capello's Milan at the summit of Serie A. Both sides had the x-factor about them and both could boast match-winners – Milan had free-scoring George Weah and Parma had the inspirational Gianfranco Zola.

It was a very different story in Turin. The champions' title defence was looking less secure by the week and by the start of November the wheels were starting to come off. Juventus were six points off the pace following a disastrous humbling by Lazio. A four-goal Beppe Signori-inspired defeat was the *bianconeri*'s heaviest league loss in over half a century and it was followed seven days later by another – at Udinese – with future Milan star Oliver Bierhoff grabbing the winner.

Bierhoff would go on to become one of the best signings in Udinese's history, scoring 57 times in 86 appearances before joining Milan. He'd link up with Alberto Zaccheroni once again at the San Siro.

After Bierhoff had seen off the champions, serious question marks were beginning to hover over them. Incredibly Juventus would fail to win away from home in Serie A for four months to leave their dreams of back-to-back Serie A titles in tatters. The only silver lining in that run was avenging their two derby defeats to Torino the previous season by beating their neighbours twice this time around, the first of which saw them handing out a five-goal thrashing, with Gianluca Vialli scoring a first-half hat-trick.

At the top though, Milan and Parma couldn't be separated and met at the Ennio Tardini stadium in mid-November. The match finished in a drab goalless draw but will always be remembered for the debut of one Gianluigi Buffon – he was drafted in as a late replacement for the injured Luca Bucci and put in a man-of-the-match performance to earn his side a point.

Baggio, Weah, Savićević – they were all frustrated time and again by the stand-in keeper. Parma though would slip behind Milan in the run-up to Christmas, winning just one of their next five fixtures while the league leaders powered on. A stunning winner from George Weah at Lazio was symptomatic of the ruthless machine that this new Milan was becoming and by the end of 1995 – despite a late wobble courtesy of three consecutive draws – they were still top. But a new challenger was emerging, a team who were in the form of their lives.

In only their second season back in Serie A, Fiorentina were flying. They now lay just a point off the leaders after suffering only one defeat in their last eight matches. The last of those came just prior to Christmas, as they took on Fabio Capello's men and shared four goals at the Artemio Franchi stadium.

Despite being held at Roma in their first match of 1996 –in which Fiorentina had come from 2–0 down to salvage a draw – they were keeping very much on Milan's coat tails.

They were coached by a man who would go on to become a huge favourite – and a title-winner against all the odds in England some 20 years later. Claudio Ranieri had assembled a side packed with talent – full of goals but with the stamp of quality from one to eleven.

Goalkeeper Francesco Toldo would become a fans' favourite at the Artemio Franchi stadium. He joined following relegation from Serie A in 1993 and would stay for the club's immediate return to the top flight and upcoming success both at home and in Europe, as well as regularly featuring for the national side in later years.

Just in front of him the likes of local boy Daniele Carnasciali and Lorenzo Amoruso took their places in one of Serie A's most watertight defences. But it wasn't just at the back that Fiorentina were impressive. The signing of Portuguese international Rui Costa from Benfica added a completely new dimension to the side in midfield and with club talisman Gabriel Batistuta ever-reliable up front Ranieri's men were a new force in the Italian game.

After their incredible first half to the season, which had the club just a point behind leaders Milan, the *viola* would hit a slump in form which ultimately cost them any chance of title glory. However, the 1995/96 season would be a hugely successful one for the team from Tuscany. Not only would they claim a fifth Coppa Italia crown but they would be back playing European football, just two years on from their promotion back to the top flight of Italian football.

A run of just two wins in nine Serie A matches derailed Fiorentina's dreams of a first scudetto since 1969 as Fabio Capello's men powered on. There was simply no stopping them. After the previous year's crushing disappointments both at home and in Europe – where the *rossoneri* had lost the title to Juventus as well as the Champions League Final to Ajax – it was normal service resumed. Most wins, fewest defeats, second highest goals scored behind Zdeněk Zeman's prolific Lazio – not to mention the best defensive record by quite some distance. But their glorious season would be tinged with sadness with the news that the architect of all of this – coach Fabio Capello – would be leaving at the end of campaign for Real Madrid.

They secured the title with two games to spare and fittingly it came against Fiorentina – their long-term rivals in the race for the scudetto. A year on from a rare trophyless season, Fabio Capello's men had bounced back in style, thanks in no small part to former World Footballer of the Year Roberto Baggio. It was fitting that he would seal the title against the club where he made his name.

It had always looked a huge risk for Juventus not to offer him a long-term contract and after his highly publicised switch to the red half of the San Siro the *bianconeri* were left to rue that decision. Baggio was voted the fans player of the year after overcoming an early season injury and became only the sixth player in Serie A history to win the title in successive years with different clubs.

So where did it all go wrong for the champions? A wretched start saw them lose four of their first 13 games, during which time the *bianconeri* dropped 18 points out of 39. Add to that almost four months without an away win and those statistics alone tell the story. The disappointment wasn't just confined to the league though as their defence of the Coppa Italia ended early too, following defeat at Atalanta.

Despite that poor start, the champions would go on a great run of form in 1996, losing just two of their last 19 league games as they finished in second place. Despite a lack of domestic success, it'd still be a glorious end to the season for Marcello Lippi's side, who were carrying Italian hopes in the Champions League.

After a great run – seeing off the likes of Borussia Dortmund and Real Madrid – Juventus would face defending champions Ajax in the final. However, with the match being held in Rome, home advantage could make the difference.

Notwithstanding the importance of the match, it had special significance for Juventus. Their only previous title in the competition just over a decade earlier had meant little, coming as it did in tragic circumstances at Heysel Stadium in Brussels where 32 out of the 39 fans to tragically lose their lives were *bianconeri.* There was thus a steely determination within the club to claim a second title that would be remembered for the right reasons.

In the final, they got the dream start. Fabrizio Ravanelli steered the Old Lady ahead from the tightest of angles but Jari Litmanen's strike shortly before half time made it 1–1. It remained level and with no further goals before or after extra time it went to penalties. After misses from future Juventus star Edgar Davids as well as Sonny Silooy, up stepped Vladimir Jugović to seal glory for Marcello Lippi's side. It was quite a way for the midfielder to crown his first season with the *bianconeri*, and it brought unbridled joy for everyone connected with the club be they players, staff or fans.

The month of May would see some notable departures from Serie A. After four seasons in Turin, Gianluca Vialli would be heading to the Premier League and Chelsea as new boss Ruud Gullit shaped his squad for the 1996/97 season. He joined on a free transfer due to a new law which had just come into effect – the Bosman ruling. This allowed any player whose contract had expired to join another club in Europe without the selling club receiving a penny, meaning contracts and their lengths were now a huge issue in football.

The big farewell though took place at the San Siro on 12 May 1996 as Fabio Capello waved goodbye to Milan at the end of a trophy-laden five years. It had included an unbeaten debut season as coach, four league titles, three Champions League Final appearances – one of which saw the *rossoneri* crush Barcelona 4–0, with a simply breathtaking performance. At the time, it was the Catalan club's heaviest defeat in European competition.

Milan marked the coach's farewell with one of their greatest performances under Fabio Capello. Relegated Cremonese were the lambs to the slaughter as the champions ended their coach's reign with a 7–1 annihilation of their already-relegated opponents. It was the club's joint biggest win under Capello. The previous record had been against Foggia, when Milan recovered from a 2–1 half-time deficit to score seven unanswered second-half goals to complete their "invincible" season.

Four years on from that it was time for the coach to say farewell as he left the San Siro pitch in tears. He was off to Real Madrid for his next challenge – and his magic touch would stay with him in the Spanish capital.

Across town it had been yet another under-achieving campaign for city rivals Inter. Paul Ince's debut season got off to a less than impressive start. Defeat by Napoli meant the end for coach Ottavio Bianchi – ironically it came at the club where he'd won the scudetto back in 1987. His replacement was Luis Suárez, appointed in a caretaker role. He'd previously enjoyed a legendary career with the club as a player back in the 1960s, when he became the world's most expensive footballer at the time after joining from Barcelona for £100,000.

Despite some promising performances, the team were struggling and towards the end of October, new President Moratti appointed Roy Hodgson, who became only the third English coach in the club's history and would be joining compatriot Paul Ince at the San Siro.

Despite having next to no experience as a professional player, Hodgson had built up quite a reputation with some of the lesser lights of European football. After leading both Halmstad and Malmö to spells of unprecedented success in the Swedish first division, people started to take notice.

Although Malmö offered the Englishman a job for life it wasn't enough to tempt Hodgson – he was ready for a new challenge and that came in Switzerland – a country where he would make his name. Neuchâtel Xamax had been highly impressed by what he had done in Scandinavia and appointed him as coach in the summer of 1990. He'd soon led the club into European competition as his achievements continued to gain international attention. His next move would see the whole of European football take notice.

The Swiss national team hadn't qualified for a major international competition since 1966 and were desperate to change that. In Roy Hodgson they saw the man to deliver it– and with him speaking both French and German it looked a match made in heaven.

Hodgson oversaw the country's qualification for the 1994 World Cup, the highlight of which undoubtedly was taking four points off Italy. Not only that, they rose to third in the FIFA world rankings, the highest the country has ever been.

With such an impressive CV Inter were the first of the European heavyweights to take a chance on Hodgson. He joined with the club languishing in mid-table and was given a baptism of fire – facing Lazio before leading his side into what was the 234th Milan derby. After earning a highly creditable draw against the league leaders he steadied the ship, aided by an impressive debut season in Italy for fellow Englishman Paul Ince.

Ince, known as the "Guvnor" – despite only scoring three goals – became a huge favourite with the fans through his all-action, committed displays, the highlight being a stunning overhead kick during an 8–2 rout of relegation-bound Padova. Ince's debut season in Italy helped the club to UEFA Cup qualification, the highlight being victory over champions-elect Milan, in the process ending the *rossoneri*'s 19-match unbeaten run in Serie A.

Despite all this they still had some way to go to catch their city rivals. Milan ultimately won the 1995/96 scudetto by eight points as departing coach Fabio Capello headed to the Spanish capital. As for the club he was leaving, the golden era was about to come to a crashing end. It was all change in Milan ... and in Turin too as the shift of power in Serie A was about to take another turn.

5

CHANGING OF THE GUARD

There was much conjecture as to who would be replacing Fabio Capello on the Milan bench for the 1996/97 season. In the end, the club hierarchy surprised the whole of Italy by appointing Uruguayan Óscar Tabárez. He'd earned his reputation in South America with both Boca Juniors and the Uruguayan national side.

In 1994, he joined Cagliari and led them to a highly creditable ninth place. Milan would be his biggest coaching job in Europe and he'd be joining the reigning champions with the near-impossible task of carrying on where Fabio Capello had left off. Quite a tall order for a coach with such little experience of European football.

Fabio Capello had just led the club to four scudetti in five seasons but that golden era had reached its conclusion – and there would be wholesale changes to the squad ahead of the new campaign. The likes of Gianluigi Lentini (to Atalanta) and Christian Panucci (to join Capello at Real Madrid) left while promising young talent like Patrick Vieira were moved on – that departure in particular would be one the club would soon regret. He surprisingly only played two games in their title-winning season and would soon be moving onto great things with Arsenal. The quality of the replacements was questionable. None of them had any Serie A experience – and it showed. The Dutch pair of Michael Reiziger (Panucci's replacement at right back) and Edgar Davids arrived from Ajax. Frenchman Christophe Dugarry arrived from Bordeaux as well as Jesper Blomqvist from Gothenburg. The language barrier was a problem as they all struggled to settle.

It was a very different story over in Turin where the contrast between Torino and new European champions Juventus couldn't have been starker. Despite losing Gianluca Vialli to Chelsea there were several replacements lined up. Up front Christian Vieri joined from Atalanta along with centre back Paolo Montero – and it'd be Vieri in particular who'd make a big impact over the following nine months. Alen Bokšić also arrived from Lazio, but all of these additions were trumped by the biggest signing of the window in Italy – the purchase of Zinedine Zidane from Bordeaux for a shade over £3 million. It was a master stroke.

Across town at Torino there was recrimination and regret. Some 12 months on from doing the league double over Juventus, Torino would find themselves relegated to Serie B for only the second time in over three decades after a disastrous campaign which had yielded just six wins. They'd be joined in the second tier by Padova, Cremonese and Bari. The southern side shipped a massive 71 goals in their 34 matches which was the key factor in their demise, as they were the top scorers in the bottom half thanks in no small part to Igor Protti. He ended the season with 24 goals and shared the top-scorer title with Beppe Signori.

Coming up were one of the sleeping giants of Italian football – Bologna. The *rossoblu* were Serie A champions seven times before the Second World War but had been languishing in the lower echelons of Italian football for far too long. Under the hugely experienced Renzo Ulivieri they were back among the big boys and with a hugely experienced squad featuring the likes of former Milan keeper Francesco Antonioli, Igor Shalimov and Giancarlo Marocchi in midfield, while up front there was no shortage of options either. Swedish international striker Kennet Andersson, Igor Kolyvanov as well as former UEFA Cup-winner Davide Fontolan were among the summer arrivals. This was not a team coming to Serie A to make up the numbers. Joining them in Serie A would be Emilian rivals Reggiana – back after a year in the second tier – as well as Perugia and Verona.

As ever there was plenty of movement in the summer transfer market. Inter signed Kanu from Ajax. Fresh from starring in – and captaining – Nigeria's gold medal-winning squad at the summer Olympics his San Siro career would prove to be short-lived due to a serious heart defect. By the time he had recovered and was ready for first team football again he'd moved on – to Arsenal. By way of replacement Inter had added Chilean striker Iván Zamorano from Real Madrid for £2.25 million.

Down in the capital, Lazio were busy strengthening their attacking options. In came Pavel Nedvěd from Sparta Prague – signed off the back of his sensational summer performances for the Czech national side in Euro '96. Joining him would be Igor Protti from relegated Bari, meaning Zdeněk Zeman's side boasted Serie A's top scorers from the previous season.

As for Roma, there was a new man in the hot seat. Argentine Carlos Bianchi was the surprising choice and he would join compatriot Abel Balbo in the eternal city.

There was a change of coach at Parma too. Nevio Scala – who'd presided over the most successful period in the club's history (during which time they'd won the Coppa Italia, Cup Winners' Cup, UEFA Cup as well as the European Super Cup), was replaced by an up-and-coming manager by the name of Carlo Ancelotti, taking on his first assignment as a Serie A coach. Ancelotti would go on to great things in future years but his appointment was a risky choice by Parma.

The season started in explosive fashion for Parma with a 3–0 rout of Napoli, with Gianfranco Zola scoring an absolute screamer. It was played on a Saturday night as Pay TV's power in Italian football broadcasting tightened its grip further. Matches were now being televised on a Saturday evening – and with there being another big game scheduled on a Sunday evening, it meant there were just five or six matches in the regular Sunday afternoon slot in which to select our live game.

Our first port of call on *Football Italia* was the San Siro for the first match of Milan's defence of the title. It was a match that would feature arguably one of the best goals scored in Serie A history.

Milan came from a goal down to beat Verona. With the champions 2–1 up and with 85 minutes on the clock, Verona were awarded a corner. What happened next is the stuff of legend. George Weah controlled it and then proceeded to run from inside the Milan penalty box the entire length of the field before firing coolly past Attilio Gregori.

Stunning as it was, it didn't make my job any easier! While there was much excitement coming from the gallery downstairs it meant the analysis had to be quickly re-edited and the closing montage completely changed as it was now all about George Weah and not newly promoted Verona giving the champions a scare on day one. Things were about to get even more problematic as Milan weren't finished yet. When Roberto Baggio added a fourth in added time, things went from busy to manic!

While Verona were eventually blown away by Milan there were a few shocks on the first day of the new campaign. Juventus were held to a 1–1 draw by Reggiana, Christian Vieri scoring on his league debut for the club.

There were far bigger surprises in store though. Despite finishing second and third in the previous two seasons Lazio's campaign got off to a shocking start. Beaten by newly promoted Bologna, they followed it up with a home defeat to Udinese.

Fiorentina were also struggling. The opening day saw them turned over at home by Vicenza with star striker Marcelo Otero grabbing all four goals. The *viola* would win just one of their opening five Serie A fixtures.

Football Italia was once again at the San Siro in week two as Roy Hodgson's Inter side took on newly promoted Perugia. The visitors were another team to cause a surprise on the opening weekend, Marco Negri's strike proving enough to beat Sampdoria. Facing Inter at the San Siro though was a different prospect altogether. They'd also kicked off with a 1–0 win, as Serie A debutant Ciriaco Sforza struck the only goal at Udinese.

One goal proved enough again, this time it was Javier Zanetti with the winner as Inter maintained their 100% record. They sat at the top alongside Roma and the early-season surprise package Bologna – who after two games were still to concede.

But how about the champions? After that impressive comeback against Verona they would soon suffer their first defeat at Sampdoria.

In week three *Football Italia* paid a first ever trip to the Dall'Ara stadium in Bologna, as the home side looked to make it three wins out of three against the champions. Goals from Marco Simone and George Weah would see Milan take maximum points, but what of the other title favourites?

Juventus recorded back-to-back wins – against Cagliari and Perugia – to move joint top. Down in the capital, Roma also boasted a 100% record and went into the home clash with Sampdoria full of confidence. After Abel Balbo put them in front it seemed like they were going to maintain their perfect start. What followed was extraordinary as the visitors struck four times in the final 25 minutes, and it was the match which would see the birth of a future star of Italian football.

Vincenzo Montella had struck 21 goals for Genoa the previous season, which unfortunately didn't prove to be enough for the side to return to Serie A, so Sampdoria paid £4 million for him to move across the city. The season would witness he and Roberto Mancini strike up a prolific partnership front for the club – the vast experience of the Sampdoria captain intertwined with the raw talent of Montella would see them score 37 Serie A goals between them, with Montella getting more than half of that figure in his debut top-flight season.

Against Roma, Montella struck twice and Mancini once as the visitors ran riot at the Stadio Olimpico. Sampdoria were sending a message to the rest of Serie A that this side's attacking capabilities would be causing plenty of headaches for defences.

By mid-October, the table was beginning to have a familiar look to it. Juventus sat one point clear at the top with Milan in second. Our next live game saw the *Football Italia* cameras pay a visit to the Romeo Menti stadium in Vicenza.

In just their second season back in the big time the home side were causing upsets once again. Already in the opening month they'd won in Florence and hit another four past Atalanta. This, though, would prove their sternest test so far as one of the favourites for the title – Juventus – headed to town.

It must've been a bit of a shock for the *Football Italia* viewers. They were used to seeing some of the iconic stadia in world football every week – the vast San Siro, the magnificent Stadio Olimpico, the cavernous Stadio delle Alpi. In contrast, the Romeo Menti stadium was a very old-school, almost English-type ground with the fans very close to the pitch. A capacity of just 12,000. No running track, no frills and one stand-out feature...

The main camera position was situated in the only covered stand and given how old it was there was a large supporting pillar in it, resulting in a restricted view at one end of the pitch. It was certainly an eye-opener for all of us!

The game more than made up for the somewhat unique surroundings as Vicenza caused yet another upset, beating the Turin giants 2–1 with Marcelo Otero claiming his fifth goal of the season. The result meant we had seven clubs separated by just two points at the top of the table, which was now led by Roy Hodgson's unbeaten Inter.

The following week saw the season's first heavyweight contest as Inter travelled to Juventus. They'd ultimately suffer a first defeat of the season as goals from Jugović and Zidane sent the Old Lady top. It'd be the Frenchman's first goal in a *bianconeri* jersey, which would prompt comparisons with Michel Platini. He'd won it all with the club in the '80s – two titles, a European Cup, a Coppa Italia as well as being named World Footballer of the Year. These Zidane/Platini comparisons would grow week by week.

The reigning champions were beginning to have a rough time of it, however. Milan had just suffered a disastrous 3–0 defeat at Roma which would signal the start of a run of just one win in seven matches, culminating in a disastrous loss at Piacenza. That defeat would result in the removal of coach Óscar Tabárez.

In came Arrigo Sacchi. Five months after Italy's disastrous European Championship campaign and five years after he left the club following huge success both at home and in Europe, he was now presiding over a Milan side in crisis. His first game would see the club crash out of the Champions League after a calamitous home defeat to Norwegian minnows Rosenborg.

The *rossoneri*'s title defence and season now lay in tatters. Seven points behind leaders Juventus, out of the Champions League and they'd soon be out of the Coppa Italia too, beaten on away goals by eventual winners Vicenza. There would be plenty more disasters still to come though as we moved into the New Year.

At Parma things weren't great either. Four consecutive matches without a win at the Ennio Tardini stadium, including three consecutive goalless draws, wasn't what the fans were used to and in the midst of it all things came to head as their star player called it quits.

Gianfranco Zola had become disillusioned with the tactics of new coach Carlo Ancelotti and his reluctance to adapt from his regimented 4–4–2 system. When Chelsea came in he saw it as too good an opportunity to turn down and off he went to London.

As we headed towards Christmas the table had an ominous look to it. Juventus were slowly moving up the gears. There resurgence was exemplified by their clash with Verona in week 13. The visitors stunned the league leaders by racing into a two-goal lead thanks to two goals from Filippo Maniero but there was a certain inevitability about what happened next. The home side – inspired by Alessandro Del Piero – fought back to win 3–2 with the winner being a contender for goal of the season from Juve's mercurial number ten.

On the same day, Inter and Sampdoria met at the San Siro in front of the *Football Italia* cameras and the viewers were treated to a seven-goal thriller as the visitors came back from 3–1 down to win 4–3. Roberto Mancini caused yet more drama in the edit suite with a winner deep into added time.

The result saw Inter slip further and further away from the league leaders. Roy Hodgson's side would fail to win any of their six Serie A matches before Christmas as they fell eight points off the pace. Paul Ince was having a good season personally, though, as was exemplified by his goal in Turin as Inter gained revenge for their recent league defeat against Juventus, seeing them off comfortably in the Coppa Italia.

Juve's closest challengers at Christmas were the two sides who would later contest the Coppa Italia final – Napoli and Vicenza. For the clubs from Milan and Rome it'd be a pretty forgettable end to 1996.

While Juventus would have enjoyed their Christmas and New Year break, a tough road still lay ahead – and just like in their title triumph two years earlier the first match of the New Year would be a trip to Parma.

This time though there would be no repeat of their memorable victory in 1995 as Enrico Chiesa's second-minute strike won it for the home side. It came courtesy of an uncharacteristic error from Angelo Peruzzi – and the match was a certainly an ill-tempered affair which saw both teams astonishingly reduced to nine men.

On the same day Inter finally returned to winning ways, thanks in no small part to Youri Djorkaeff's incredible acrobatic strike which put his side on the way to a 3–1 win over Roma. It was a goal so good that he even got congratulated by referee Graziano Cesari.

Across town at Milan things were getting progressively worse. A 3–0 defeat at Lazio heaped yet more misery on the club as Arrigo Sacchi's return was getting more disastrous by the week.

Away from the crisis at Milan, all of a sudden we had a title race. Seven days after their defeat in Parma, Juventus dropped more points as Atalanta held them to a goalless draw in Turin. Sampdoria had drawn level with Inter in second place as the gap to Juventus was now down to just two points.

Meanwhile, in the capital both Lazio and Roma would have both loved to have Juve's problems. The two sides were marooned in mid-table and both would be about to lose patience with their coaches.

Lazio's home defeat by Bologna was one too many for club President Sergio Cragnotti and he called on Dino Zoff for a second spell in charge, as his patience with Zdeněk Zeman had finally run out. As for Roma, it was soon time to say goodbye to Carlos Bianchi and like their city rivals they called upon a former coach. Sweden's Nils Liedholm returned to the club he'd coached to the European Cup Final back in 1984.

While Dino Zoff would guide Lazio to fourth place and UEFA Cup qualification – it was a very different story across town. Under Liedholm Roma would only win one of their final eight fixtures as they'd finish in their lowest league position since 1979 – ending up just four points above the relegation zone.

At the top it was beginning to look like a two-way shoot-out between Juventus and Parma for the title and as April began we came to a pivotal weekend. In the *Football Italia* live game Parma swept Sampdoria aside to move within three points of the leaders, who faced a tough game at Milan in the evening.

At least it looked that way on paper. Some 11 months on from the *rossoneri* claiming their 15th scudetto, the champions' title defence lay in ruins. Sitting 13 points behind Juventus following a quite disastrous campaign they were about to hit rock-bottom, as Marcello Lippi's side would inflict upon the *rossoneri* a record Serie A defeat, scoring a staggering six times at the San Siro. Marco Simone's volley counted for nothing as Milan were ripped apart time and again.

Despite following that up with a shock 3–0 home defeat by Udinese the following week – during which Juventus missed two penalties – Marcello Lippi and his side were inching ever closer to a second title in three seasons and just like in 1995 they had the chance to seal it against Parma.

With three games left, the champions-elect had a six-point advantage knowing a win would clinch it. However, a defeat would make things very interesting indeed over the last couple of games.

In the end, the match was an anti-climax as it ended 1–1, leaving Juventus just a point away from the title. With their upcoming Champions League Final against Borussia Dortmund, Juventus would play their final away game – at Atalanta – on the Friday evening as *Gazzetta Football Italia* was being edited. As some of the team went upstairs to watch the game we discovered to our horror that it was being recorded with the timecode in vision which was hastily removed just before Filippo Inzaghi scored his 22nd goal of the season to put the home side ahead.

Early in the second half Mark Iuliano chose the perfect time to score his first Serie A goal and that was enough for the point Juventus needed as they were crowned champions of Italy for the 24th time.

Though it may not have been celebrated on the field with emotion and unbridled joy, it was still a huge moment in the club's history. While the goals of the departed Gianluca Vialli and Fabrizio Ravanelli (who'd joined Middlesbrough the previous summer) were missed, this time it was a real collective effort. Vieri, Del Piero and the much-travelled Michele Padovano contributed 24 between them. Zidane and Jugović scored 12 from midfield. Couple that with a miserly defence (just 24 goals conceded) and that was why they were champions.

Juventus ending up losing to Borussia Dortmund in Munich so missed out on a league and Champions League double, but there was still a feeling of elation in Turin. A year on from losing the title to Milan, the *bianconeri* were back at the summit of Italian football and once again a dominant force in Europe too. The question everyone was asking was could they stay there this time?

Up at Milan there were plenty of recriminations. The *rossoneri* – under Arrigo Sacchi – had finished down in 11th place, just six points above the relegation zone after a disastrous title defence.

The end of the 1996/97 season would also be an emotional one for the club as after well over 500 Serie A appearances captain Franco Baresi called time on his playing career. A one-club man, his career had seen him win an incredible 17 titles, consisting of six scudetti, four Italian Super Cups (Serie A's version of the Community Shield), three Champions League titles, two UEFA Super Cups and two Intercontinental Cups. It was a truly incredible haul and as his career drew to a close the club wanted to express due respect for his achievements – their classy gesture was to retire his number six shirt.

Roy Hodgson and Inter would end the season in third place, as they narrowly finished behind Parma in the race for Champions League qualification. It had been a period of improvement under their English coach, signing off their season with just one defeat in ten matches, and they still had their UEFA Cup Final against Schalke to look forward to.

Back then it was a two-legged affair and despite losing 1–0 in Germany everyone still expected Inter to claim a third title of the decade in this competition. Iván Zamorano levelled the tie and that's the way it stayed until the end of extra time, so the final would go to penalties for only the third time in the competition's history. After misses from Zamorano and Aron Winter it was Schalke who would win their first European title.

It would prove to be the end of the line for Hodgson. The home fans let him know their thoughts as missiles rained down onto the San Siro turf. He was heading back to England – and Blackburn Rovers.

As the 1996/97 season came to a close there were still some wonderful moments to savour. Vicenza claimed the biggest prize in their history, beating Napoli 3–1 on aggregate to win the Coppa Italia, qualifying for Europe for only the second time.

Two goals on the final day ensured Atalanta's Pippo Inzaghi finished as the league's top scorer. He would soon be off to Juventus.

A 3–0 win at Roma ensured Udinese would be in the UEFA Cup at the end of just their second season back in Serie A.

The campaign would wind down in the most dramatic style as Piacenza and Cagliari met in a relegation play-off in Naples. The match ended in a 3–1 win for Piacenza and the Sardinians' seven-year stay in Serie A was over. They were joined in Serie B by Verona, Reggiana and Perugia – all heading down after just one season back in the top flight.

The summer of 1997 was – in true *calcio* style – busy. There were transfers, the usual coaching merry-go-round but the whole of Italy and indeed Europe were only talking about one deal – Ronaldo's transfer from Barcelona to Inter.

Ronaldo – or to give him his full name Ronaldo Luís Nazário da Lima – was the hottest property in world football and after months of chasing Barcelona for his services Massimo Moratti had finally got his man.

After scoring an incredible 76 times in his previous three seasons with PSV and Barcelona he was seen as the man to take Inter to their first scudetto since 1989. Blessed with incredible strength, lightning pace and lethal finishing, the Brazilian signed for Inter for a world record £20 million. He would later become only the second man – after Diego Maradona – to break the record twice.

Ronaldo – dubbed *il fenomeno* by the Italian press – would not be joining Paul Ince at the San Siro though, as the Englishman had returned home, signing for Liverpool for £4 million. There were plenty of other changes in the blue half of the San Siro. They'd signed an unheard-of Uruguayan forward by the name of Álvaro Recoba, who'd never played in Europe. As time went on he'd make an impression to almost rival his more illustrious fellow South American.

With Roy Hodgson gone, Massimo Moratti needed to find a coach. There were plenty of candidates but in the end he appointed Luigi Simoni, and while his only experience of managing a big club had been at Napoli 12 months earlier, he proved to be hugely popular among the players and supporters.

In his first training session he introduced himself, saying what an honour it was for him to work with such a star-studded squad. Ronaldo was joining players of the highest quality – and the squad had very much a South American flavour to it.

Javier Zanetti – equally comfortable on the right side of defence or midfield – would go on to have a stellar career with the club – a period that would last 19 years and over 600 appearances. Not only that, he'd amass 143 appearances for his country during which time he'd become the most capped player in Argentinian history.

Zanetti's compatriot Diego Simeone signed in the summer of 1997 from Atlético Madrid. Another international star who'd make over a century of appearances for the national team, he'd also experience a hugely successful two years with the club.

Then there was Chilean striker Iván Zamorano, who'd also been a legend for club and country. He'd made his name with Real Madrid, scoring 77 times in 137 appearances before heading to the San Siro.

Álvaro Recoba would become a club legend too. Not much was known of him outside of Uruguay but the 1997/98 season would see him make his mark with some remarkable goals. Add in the likes of Youri Djorkaeff as well as domestic talent such as Gianluca Pagliuca, Maurizio Ganz, Marco Branca and Francesco Moriero and it was clear the new coach had a squad that had every chance of challenging for the scudetto.

Simoni had made his name among some of the lesser lights of Serie A, and in particular Cremonese where he'd kept the minnows in the division against the odds, before he moved south to Napoli, and come within touching distance of winning the Coppa Italia. The challenge at Inter though would be the biggest job of his career by quite some distance.

The 1997/98 season was preceded by plenty of activity both in the transfer market and on the coaching front. On the other side of the San Siro, Arrigo Sacchi was fired and back came Fabio Capello after guiding Real Madrid to the La Liga title. After falling out with President Lorenzo Sanz, he left Spain to return home.

After having a disastrous time of it under Sacchi and Óscar Tabárez, better times were expected in the red half of Milan. This side though was a pale shadow of that which had previously swept all before them under Capello and before the season began he was about to lose his star man.

The new boss made it pretty clear that Roberto Baggio wasn't part of his plans so a transfer to Parma was agreed. However, coach Carlo Ancelotti astonishingly didn't want him either. Like Zola before him he didn't feel the two-time title-winner would fit into his regimented 4–4–2 system, so in the end he signed for ambitious Bologna. Renzo Ulivieri's side had narrowly missed out on European qualification upon their return to Serie A and weren't prepared to rest on their laurels. Baggio would prove to be a stellar signing as during the course of the season he'd turn the clock back with some inspirational performances, culminating in a return to the national side in time for the World Cup.

At the top, there were also changes afoot at Juventus. The *bianconeri*'s policy of selling stars and replacing them would continue to bear fruit. Christian Vieri was transferred to Atlético Madrid for almost £16 million as Juventus made a £12 million profit on the forward in 12 months. The money was used to snap up the previous season's top scorer in Serie A – Filippo Inzaghi from Atalanta. He'd be joined in Turin by fellow forward Daniel Fonseca and Dutch midfielder Edgar Davids.

In the capital the biggest shock was the move of Zdeněk Zeman. The Czech had coached Lazio for much of the previous campaign but would now controversially be taking the hotseat at bitter rivals Roma.

There was a new coach at Lazio too. Sven-Göran Eriksson – who'd enjoyed five largely successful seasons with Sampdoria – headed south and he'd be joined by his captain Roberto Mancini who said farewell too.

He'd spent 15 years in Genoa, during which time he'd won a scudetto, four Coppa Italia titles, the Italian Super Cup as well as the Cup Winners' Cup – but he now had a new challenge and he'd be adding plenty more silverware in the capital.

The season started in late August and as it kicked off *Football Italia* commentator Peter Brackley was a worried man. We were on air a mere 12 or so hours after the news broke of the tragic death of Princess Diana. Our first match would be Ronaldo's debut as newly promoted Brescia visited the San Siro.

On the right side of the visitors' defence would be youth product Aimo Diana and in the circumstances Brackers didn't know whether he could mention him by name.

"Is it insensitive to mention him? ... Shall I call him the Brescia right back? ... Shall I just ignore him completely and not mention him at all?"

In the end, the consensus was to just carry on as he normally would on what would turn into a dramatic opening day. There would be no debut goal for Inter's star acquisition and it'd be a less high-profile signing to steal the headlines.

Just before Dario Hubner's turn and finish had fired Brescia into a shock lead on 73 minutes Luigi Simoni brought on Álvaro Recoba and the Uruguayan forward turned the match on its head, firing home a 25-yard rocket before finding the other top corner with a stunning free kick as Inter got off to a winning start on a dramatic day at the San Siro.

It was a dazzling start to life in Serie A for Recoba but he wasn't the only debutant to score on the opening day as Roberto Mancini, Pippo Inzaghi and Roberto Baggio were all on target too. The performance of the opening weekend though came from Fiorentina's Gabriel Batistuta who struck a hat-trick at Udinese, the last goal of which was an incredible acrobatic effort as the *viola* struck twice in the last four minutes to turn defeat into victory.

Ronaldo did get up and running the following week though, as he once again featured on *Football Italia*, inspiring Inter to a 4–2 win at Bologna. That'd be the first of four in three games for the Brazilian as Inter boasted a 100% record after four games.

Across town Milan were only out of the relegation zone on goal difference. The home defeat to Vicenza coming after a particularly poor performance as Fabio Capello watched on in disbelief. Things would get even worse though in their next home game though as newly promoted Lecce – who'd lost all of their first five matches – beat Milan at the San Siro for the first time in their history. A subsequent nine-match unbeaten run would soon steady the ship and ease the pressure on their beleaguered coach.

What of the chasing pack though? Parma, Juventus and Roma were all unbeaten after five matches and just two points behind Inter, and all three had shown flashes of brilliance over the opening month or so. Roma's 6–2 rout of Napoli was a statement of intent and top marksman Abel Balbo was on fire, scoring six times in the opening five rounds.

Their opponents though would be facing one of the bleakest seasons in their illustrious history. For the first time in over 30 years Napoli would be on their way down to Serie B following an horrendous campaign that would yield just two wins and a pitiful 14 points.

That annihilation in the capital would mean the end for new coach Bortolo Mutti – he'd be the first of four coaches at the San Paolo as Corrado Ferlaino's 30th year as club President would be the darkest. He'd had a stormy relationship at times with the club's supporters – among the most passionate and loyal in Italy.

While there were great periods under his leadership – none bigger than the Maradona years featuring a league and cup double in 1987 as well as another scudetto in 1990 – the numerous sales of star players such as Maradona and Dino Zoff to make ends meet didn't endear him to the *tifosi*.

While things were bleak in Naples, 900 kilometres north in Turin there was a lot more cheer. Juventus would soon click into top gear and after scoring nine goals against Bari and Udinese in consecutive weeks they were Inter's closest challengers. The second of those victories would create a fair bit of controversy as Oliver Bierhoff's lob clearly went over the line with the match still goalless. Juventus would go on to win the match 4–1 and there would be plenty more contentious incidents in the months ahead!

However, a succession of unexpected draws towards the end of the year had enabled Inter to open up a four-point lead at the top and steaming up behind them and Juventus were the aforementioned Udinese who went into Christmas on the back of a phenomenal win over Inter. Oliver Bierhoff's stunning header in added time moved his side to within four points of the league leaders. It was the culmination of a run which had brought five wins in six matches since that controversial defeat in Turin.

Despite that setback, things were going very smoothly for Luigi Simoni's Inter but before the end of the calendar year they would be rocked by some tragic news, with the passing of legendary coach Helenio Herrera. After a fairly undistinguished playing career – during which he turned out for some of the lesser lights in European football – he moved into coaching in his mid-30s just after the end of the Second World War. He would make his name in Spain, coaching a number of top clubs which culminated in him being named as Barcelona boss. He would win two league titles at the Camp Nou before moving to Italy and Inter. His eight years in Milan would be among the most successful in the club's history as his side won no fewer than three league titles as well as two European Cups.

It was a golden period for the club as Inter swept all before them, but they would draw more than their fair amount of criticism. He introduced an infamous tactic by the name of *catenaccio.* This tactic (its literal meaning "door bolt") is still talked about to this day. The system involved four defenders man-marking the opposing attackers with the idea that an extra player – a sweeper or *libero* – would pick up any loose ball that a defender couldn't reach. While it worked for *Il Grande Inter* in the '60s it was unpopular abroad and branded too negative. It worked for the *nerazzurri* though. The trophies continued to pile up at home and abroad. However, in the 1967 European Cup Final, Inter – going for a hat-trick of wins in this prestigious competition – were shocked by Celtic, losing 2–1 to the Scottish club, despite scoring early on. That loss brought the glorious era to an end. Inter wouldn't taste glory in this competition again for over 40 years.

Things were going pretty well for the club in the battle for the 1997/98 scudetto though, and 1998 would start with the game of the season so far, as Inter hosted Juventus at the San Siro. The top-of-the-table showdown was preceded by the presentation of the World Footballer of the Year trophy to Ronaldo – and despite it being a night match our *Football Italia* viewers were able to enjoy the occasion as the top two went head to head – with just a point separating them.

Channel 4's commitment to *Football Italia* was illustrated as we showed other live matches away from Serie A too. Both legs of Italy's World Cup qualifying play-off with Russia were broadcast – the first of which saw James and guests shivering in the Moscow snow – and we also had live coverage of both legs of Lazio's UEFA Cup semi-final against Atlético Madrid.

This showed how much Channel 4 valued transmitting what was then the best league in Europe, but that scudetto showdown between Inter and Juventus was the most special, in a primetime slot on a Saturday evening.

Just one goal settled the match as Youri Djorkaeff tapped in Ronaldo's cross. It all enabled Inter to open up a four-point cushion at the top. However, the *nerazzurri* were about to hit some choppy waters. First, they crashed out of the Coppa Italia to bitter rivals Milan, a 5–0 mauling in the first leg (with pretty much a full-strength team) came out of the blue as the *rossoneri* cruised through 5–1 on aggregate.

A first home defeat soon followed against Bari. The southern side would prove to be something of a nemesis for Inter in the '90s. Having already trounced the *nerazzurri* 4–1 two seasons earlier, they would go on to inflict yet more pain before the end of the season.

That defeat would be followed by a disappointing 1–1 draw at Empoli, where Inter were behind for almost the entire game before being rescued by Álvaro Recoba. Not for the first time the Uruguayan got his side out of a hole as he maintained his reputation for scoring stunning goals. This one was more than special though and was arguably goal of the season – lobbing keeper Marco Roccati from over 40 yards to salvage a point.

It was harsh on Empoli who had more than matched the league leaders for long spells and it was another indicator of the progress this side had made. Having come from the third division and achieved back-to-back promotions these were golden times for the club, as they became the first Tuscan side since Pisa back in the '80s to join Fiorentina in Serie A.

The mastermind of this success was Luciano Spalletti. Tuscan born and bred, this was his first coaching job and he would guide the club to safety before being snapped up by Sampdoria. His stock would rise further in Genoa and lead to him being twice being appointed coach of Roma, as well as landing the coaching job at Inter.

As well as holding Ronaldo and Co. in that draw, Empoli would go on to cause more than a few shocks during the course of the season. They beat both Lazio and Sampdoria, and came within a whisker of getting a point off Juventus, but the highlight was undoubtedly taking four points off more illustrious Tuscan rivals Fiorentina – including a dramatic win at the Artemio Franchi stadium. They were also the highest scorers in the bottom half of the table – Lecce and Napoli both conceded five against them.

Their dogged display against Inter didn't just help them though. Juve's win on the same day over Atalanta enabled them to finally move to the top of the table, which was starting to have an ominous look to it. Juventus though were about to suffer a damaging blow to their scudetto chances, as hugely experienced defender Ciro Ferrara suffered a broken leg at Lecce during what was a routine win. It would leave Marcello Lippi without one of his most seasoned campaigners for the remainder of the season.

Even without Ferrara, Juventus kept on winning. Roma were swept aside and by mid-February Inter's title dream looked like it was slipping away. A disastrous and unexpected defeat to Bologna at the San Siro left them four points behind the defending champions and was symptomatic of their inconsistent form in the New Year. A 5–0 thrashing of relegation-bound Lecce (starring a Ronaldo hat-trick) would be followed by a three-goal loss at Lazio. A routine win over Napoli would then be followed by defeat in Parma.

Fortunately for Luigi Simoni's men they weren't losing ground as Juventus were beaten in Florence and would also be dropping points against Brescia and Udinese. A surprising 2–2 draw at home to rock-bottom Napoli followed, it was only the second time the *bianconeri* had dropped points at the Stadio delle Alpi all season.

By late March the gap in this thrilling title race was down to just one point as Juventus were held at Parma on another dramatic afternoon, before Inter gained revenge over Milan for their Coppa Italia thrashing by demolishing them 3–0 in the derby.

While Juventus and Inter were the main protagonists in this thrilling title race, all of a sudden we had a third team putting themselves very much in the picture – Lazio.

Sven-Göran Eriksson was presiding over a remarkable debut season in the capital, which would ultimately see his team fall away, but they'd win their first trophy since claiming the scudetto back in 1974. The Swede had sold talismanic striker Beppe Signori to his former club Sampdoria. In attack though the club had re-signed Alen Bokšić and could also call upon Pierluigi Casiraghi as well as the mercurial Roberto Mancini.

Lazio had put quite a run together to get into title contention. The bedrock of that was their defence as they achieved an astonishing seven consecutive clean sheets, and there was no debate about what the highlight of it was. Their 2–0 win over fierce rivals Roma in early March saw them create history, as Lazio had not only beaten the *giallorossi* home and away in the league but also in the Coppa Italia, meaning they had won all four meetings during the course of the season. To show their joy and appreciation the Lazio fans built a plaque to commemorate this remarkable feat.

Their defence was finally breached in early April though, as Juventus won at the Stadio Olimpico. Filippo Inzaghi struck the only goal as Marcello Lippi's side cleared a major hurdle on the road to the title.

A week earlier the league leaders had made another statement by thrashing Milan 4–1, but this win over Lazio was huge, but not for the first – or indeed last time during the 1997/98 season – it was shrouded in controversy.

With the *bianconeri* leading, Lazio were convinced they should have been awarded a penalty following a handball by Mark Iuliano. It left the Roman club seething as earlier in the campaign they'd gone down to defeat in Turin when there had been some questionable decisions, too.

Inter, meanwhile, were breathing down Juve's necks and the gap at the top was now down to just a point. With the sides due to face off in Turin at the end of April, the anticipation of this potentially scudetto-deciding clash was growing week by week.

Seven days before it, both teams were beginning to feel the pressure, nerves were getting frayed and there was yet more drama and controversy.

Juventus scraped past Empoli 1–0 in Tuscany but were aided by another controversial decision, which this time was a lot more clear-cut. An Empoli header looked to have crossed the line before keeper Angelo Peruzzi clawed it away. Referee Pasquale Rodomonti was unmoved though and in the days prior to goal-line technology – let alone VAR – the "goal" didn't stand as Fabio Pecchia's earlier strike proved decisive. Inter rode their luck too against Udinese – scoring twice in the last ten minutes – but not before Udinese had hit the post and been denied a clear penalty.

If anyone thought those incidents were controversial though, they would pale into insignificance seven days later, when Juventus met Inter for the match billed as the "scudetto showdown". It was a match that is still talked about to this day. Quite simply, all hell was about to break loose.

The build-up to the match had been going on for weeks. Finally, it was here at a sold-out Stadio delle Alpi where the two best sides in the land – separated by just a single point – were about to take each other on in the most thrilling and intense of title races in years.

It wasn't just in Italy that this match was being talked about. All over Europe people were captivated by this incredible duel in what was still the greatest league in the world, and what a treat the viewers were in for. In the black and white corner we had Del Piero,

Deschamps and Zidane and in the blue and black corner Djorkaeff, Simeone and Ronaldo.

The match kicked off amid a cauldron of noise and anticipation. With the scudetto on the line the nerves both on the pitch and off it were immense. Both teams knew that one mistake could potentially cost them the title. However, with 21 minutes on the clock the home side struck. Alessandro Del Piero twisted and turned in the box, almost losing possession. He didn't though and curled a shot from the tightest of angles into the far corner. Cue bedlam. It was his 21st league goal of a remarkable campaign and could prove to be his most important.

Back came Inter. Ronaldo's sheer power and strength, not to mention his pace, had the Juventus defence on the back foot but they couldn't find a way past Angelo Peruzzi in the first half.

On to the second half and one of the most talked-about 45 minutes of football in Serie A history. Inter forced Juventus back time and again as the *bianconeri* struggled to maintain control. Lippi replaced Inzaghi with the combative midfielder Antonio Conte. Simoni introduced another striker to the fray, Chilean Iván Zamorano. Juventus were more than happy to frustrate their opponents. Every foul, every free kick that went their way greeted with delirium by the raucous home supporters. In the 69th minute though, the ball dropped to Ronaldo in the penalty area and he poked it past Mark Iuliano before the Juventus defender body-checked him.

"No penalty", said referee Piero Ceccarini. He was quite possibly the only person in the stadium who genuinely thought that. The Inter players surrounded him, incandescent with rage. In the meantime, Juventus were counter-attacking. Zidane played the ball into the path of Del Piero in the box who received a shove from Taribo West, before going over theatrically. This time Ceccarini awarded the penalty.

It's quite possibly the most controversial 15 seconds in the history of Italian football. Inter had already hinted that some of the decisions Juventus had benefited from during the course of season weren't right. The Udinese goal that was clearly over the line back in November. The goal that Empoli had recently "scored" against

Juventus and not been given. A controversial handball not penalised in Juve's win at Lazio three weeks earlier that would have resulted in a penalty. And now this.

It was too much for them to take. The entire Inter team surrounded Ceccarini but he wasn't going to change his mind. Luigi Simoni was sent from the dugout, he'd called the referee "shameful".

Del Piero would be denied from the spot by Pagliuca but in the end Juventus narrowly clung on to the win that all but sealed the title, but the furore wasn't ending there. It was only just beginning. Ceccarini was besieged by reporters while exiting the Stadio delle Alpi. He was a vastly experienced referee – who two years earlier had represented the country at Euro '96. To this day he still feels he made the right decision.

The following week would see day after day devoted to this incident in the Italian newspapers, but the front page of *Gazzetta dello Sport* the following day summed it up pretty succinctly: "Ceccarini, what have you done?"

It wasn't just in the world of football that emotions were running high. Incredibly it led to fights in parliament. The following Sunday – prior to Inter's home game with Piacenza – the *interisti* unfurled a plethora of banners to register their disgust.

"Meglio secondi che ladri" (It's better to be second than thieves)
"Campioni d'onesta" (Champions of honesty)
"Vergogna" (Shame)
"Tre piccoli porcellini – Moggi/Bettega/Ceccarini" (Three little pigs – a dig at the Juventus hierarchy and their "relationship" with referees)

The following weekend was a damp squib as both sides fired a blank. Inter were held to a 0–0 draw by Piacenza and it was goalless too for Juventus in Vicenza. So, we headed to the penultimate round with Juventus still four points clear. The *bianconeri* knew a win over Bologna would be enough. Inter made the long trip south to Bari, praying for a miracle.

It was another afternoon of high drama. Juventus fought back from going a goal down to take a lead 2–1 lead, thanks to two goals from Filippo Inzaghi. Inter were ahead in the San Nicola stadium after Ronaldo's first-half goal.

But just as Juventus were in sight of the finishing line they were pegged back by the player they'd controversially let go just three years earlier. Roberto Baggio was on his way to a remarkable recall to the national side for the upcoming World Cup after a stunning first season at Bologna – and the penultimate strike of a 22-goal season came against his former employers in Turin to make it 2–2.

The title race appeared to be going to the final week but the last ten minutes in both Turin and Bari would turn out to be full of drama. First Inzaghi completed his hat-trick to put Juventus on the brink, and 1,000 kilometres south at the San Nicola stadium, Inter's scudetto dreams were about to go up in smoke.

First, substitute Nicola Ventola (who would ironically join the *nerazzurri* in the summer) struck with just four minutes remaining to bring his side level. With so little time to now win the game, Inter poured forward in a desperate bid to try to take the scudetto to the final day, but in the 89th minute they were caught napping and Phil Masinga tapped in at the far post to end their title dreams. A league campaign that had promised so much ended in tears. A first title in almost a decade had once again eluded them and while the temptation to look back a few weeks to the huge controversy against Juventus was understandable, the statistics pointed to a deserved scudetto for Juventus. Fewest defeats, most goals scored – indeed Alessandro Del Piero and Filippo Inzaghi had struck almost 40 between them.

The season wasn't over for either Juventus or Inter, though. There were European finals ahead for them both and this time it'd be Inter celebrating, as Luigi Simoni guided his side to a 3–0 win over Lazio in Paris in what was the fourth all-Italian UEFA Cup Final of the '90s. It highlighted again Serie A's dominance in this competition as Inter picked up a third success of the decade.

For Juventus though it was disappointment. Some 12 months on from losing their Champions League crown to Borussia Dortmund, they were beaten in the final again – 1–0 by Real Madrid in Amsterdam. Back-to-back Serie A titles though was no mean feat and as the season wound down there were plenty of other stories of triumph and tragedy.

As a result of Inter's second-place finish and subsequent UEFA Cup win, Italy would have four representatives in the 1998/99 UEFA Cup – Parma, Fiorentina, Roma and Udinese. For the last of those sides it was a noticeable triumph. In only their third season back in the top flight their third-place finish – inspired by the leadership of coach Alberto Zaccheroni and the goals of Serie A top scorer Oliver Bierhoff – it was a golden time for them. They would however become the victims of their own success as Zaccheroni and Bierhoff would link up at Milan just a few months later as the *rossoneri* underwent a major overhaul after a disastrous season where they'd finished tenth.

That was nothing compared to Napoli though. An horrendous year, in which the *azzurri* went down to an embarrassing 24 defeats in their 34 matches, saw the southern giants relegated to Serie B. Just a decade on from the glory days of Maradona the season would end in tears and the iconic images at the end of Napoli's defeat at Parma with five games left, of Parma's Fabio Cannavaro consoling the tearful Napoli goalkeeper Pino Taglialatela – both native Neapolitans – was one of the enduring images of the campaign.

The story of the 1997/98 season was all about Juventus though. In their centenary year Marcello Lippi's side had achieved back-to-back titles and as we headed into the summer and the World Cup the question all of *calcio* was asking was who could stop them?

6

PAIN AND GLORY

There was more penalty heartbreak in the summer of 1998 for the Italian national side. After losing to Brazil in a shoot-out in the World Cup Final four years earlier, this time it'd be eventual champions France who'd eliminate them.

As attention turned back to domestic matters there were once again wholesale changes around the division. As mentioned earlier Fabio Capello's return as coach lasted all of one season as the board sought to pursue a new strategy. Up and coming Udinese boss Alberto Zaccheroni fitted the bill perfectly – both he and Oliver Bierhoff were about to recreate their magic, but on a far bigger stage than before.

It was all change at Parma too. Carlo Ancelotti was replaced by Alberto Malesani, who'd just guided Fiorentina to a fifth-place finish. Malesani and Parma were once again busy in the transfer market. In came Abel Balbo after five hugely successful seasons with Roma, along with Diego Fuser from the blue half of the capital.

Runners-up Inter had been adding some firepower too. Fresh from his stunning season with Bologna, Roberto Baggio headed back to the San Siro, but this time wearing the blue and black of Inter. He was joined by young striker Nicola Ventola – who just a few months earlier had helped put the final nail in the *nerazzurri*'s scudetto coffin. The club had also signed a 19-year-old midfielder from Brescia by the name of Andrea Pirlo.

There were few changes in Turin as Marcello Lippi kept his faith with the squad that had just won back-to-back titles. The defending champions though would be about to suffer a dramatic fall from grace in what would be their least successful campaign since 1991 and their first trophyless one under Lippi.

Their cause wasn't helped by the distraction of a much-publicised drug trial – the allegation being that several of the Juventus players had been taking performance-enhancing drugs over the previous trophy-laden seasons. Club doctor Riccardo Agricola was given a suspended prison sentence for providing them and at the start of the 1998/99 season outspoken AS Roma coach Zdeněk Zeman stated that "football needed to get out of the pharmacy" and basically accused Juventus of cheating. The club was eventually cleared of sporting fraud.

Before the season kicked off, we had a couple of new teams for the *Football Italia* viewers to enjoy. Venezia were about to embark on a first Serie A campaign in over three decades. They'd be joined by Salernitana in the top flight. With Napoli down in Serie B, their near neighbours were eagerly anticipating a first season at this level since the 1940s.

The champions started their campaign away to newly promoted Perugia. The Umbrians made headlines of their own during the summer by signing a Japanese midfielder by the name of Hidetoshi Nakata. He'd go on to enjoy a highly successful seven years in Italy, during which time he'd win the title with Roma.

Football Italia would feature Nakata on the opening day of the new season in a quite astonishing seven-goal thriller which gave an early indication that it wouldn't necessarily be business as usual at the Serie A summit. Goals from Edgar Davids, Igor Tudor and Gianluca Pessotto saw Juventus race into a 3–0 half-time lead at the Renato Curi stadium. In the end they scraped home 4–3, as two goals from new boy Nakata made for some very uncomfortable viewing for Marcello Lippi, but Juventus clung on.

The only teams with 100% records after the opening fortnight were Milan, Fiorentina and Juventus – but out of the trio it was the reigning champions who'd looked the least convincing. After almost blowing a three-goal lead in Perugia, they then scraped past newly promoted Cagliari thanks to an own goal.

Week three would see two of them go head to head as Fiorentina travelled to the San Siro. Following Malesani's departure to Parma, club President Vittorio Cecchi Gori went for experience in the shape of legendary coach Giovanni Trapattoni, back in Serie A following his second stint with Bayern Munich.

Trapattoni's new side were off to a flier in and things were about to get even better. The *viola* would soon find themselves atop the league table after a Gabriel Batistuta hat-trick inspired them to a 3–1 win at Milan.

The same weekend saw Juve's first defeat too. Dino Baggio – who'd previously spent two years with the *bianconeri* – struck the winning goal as new coach Malesani celebrated wildly with the fans at the Ennio Tardini stadium. Amazingly Parma wouldn't actually concede until the sixth week of the season – at Perugia.

Juventus would bounce back the following week although once again it was less than convincing. Filippo Inzaghi scored the only goal early on in the match with Piacenza – more notable for the fact that he was lining up against younger brother Simone.

Fiorentina meanwhile were going from strength to strength. Edmundo's goal against Udinese in added time made it four wins from four as the fiery Brazilian opened his account for the season. He'd joined the *viola* for around £6 million and came with quite a reputation for his explosive talent. With a temperament to match, he received a large number of red cards, often for fighting on the field, as well as with team mates at training and falling out with a succession of coaches. It earned him the nickname of *"O Animal"*.

His off-the-field antics were even worse. They included giving whisky to a chimpanzee as well as causing the deaths of three people after an horrific car accident. For this he was handed a prison sentence, although he spent very little time behind bars.

His talent though was unquestionable and Fiorentina were hoping that they might be able to bring out the best in him. Nine goals in all competitions wasn't the greatest return but there were flashes of brilliance interspersed with more off-the-field problems which proved immensely frustrating for Trapattoni. The low point came when he stayed behind in Brazil during the Christmas break (after activating the "Rio carnival" clause in his contract) and returning two days late.

By mid-October the table had an unfamiliar look to it. Even though they weren't firing on all cylinders, Juventus had just beaten Inter again in Turin, were beginning to accumulate points and lay a point clear of Fiorentina, whose lightning start had just started to stall. Milan had suffered two defeats already – against Fiorentina and Cagliari – while Inter seemed to be having a hangover from their scudetto disappointment. Three straight defeats, including two at the San Siro – where they conceded five to Lazio and another three to their nemesis Bari – left them well off the pace as the *Football Italia* cameras headed to Udine. It would turn out to be the day that would destroy Juventus' dream of a hat-trick of Serie A titles.

It had all started so well for the *bianconeri*. Goals from Zidane and Inzaghi had put the champions in complete control at the Friuli stadium. Even though Jonathan Bachini pulled one back with 25 minutes remaining it seemed Marcello Lippi's side would be recording another win. But in added time came the moment that arguably cost them any chance of another scudetto.

Alessandro Del Piero – stretching to reach a volley – landed awkwardly on his left knee before falling to the ground in agony. He was immediately stretchered off. Udinese then proceeded to grab an injury-time equaliser against a shell-shocked Juventus, but that wasn't the whole story. The Juventus forward had ruptured the anterior and posterior ligaments in his left knee, an injury so serious that he would require nine months of rehabilitation. It left Juve's season in tatters as they'd fail to win any of their next five league games, astonishingly failing to even score a goal.

A 2–0 defeat at Roma started the dire run of form, a match preceded by the *giallorossi* supporters taunting their opposition about the ongoing drug investigation, as a banner in the Curva Sud stated simply "*Lippi spacciatore*" ("Lippi the drug dealer").

Defeats to Lazio and Fiorentina soon followed, but the low point was a 3–0 hammering at Bologna, with all the goals coming in the first half. By the time Juventus won again – a 3–0 defeat of Salernitana in December – they were eighth.

Things weren't going much better in Europe either. The club's Champions League campaign – in a group containing the likes of Galatasaray, Athletic Bilbao and Rosenborg – got off to an inauspicious start as draws in their opening five group matches left their qualification hopes hanging by a thread. A win over the Norwegians saw the *bianconeri* scrape through – and miraculously they managed to top the group.

The Turin giants weren't the only ones struggling though. Inter weren't faring any better either and despite scraping an ill-deserved win against struggling Salernitana the club hierarchy made the controversial decision to axe the popular Luigi Simoni. Despite the poor league form the 59-year-old had still brought Champions League football to the *nerazzurri* after finishing runners-up to Juventus. He'd also guided the club to the knockout rounds after topping a tough group featuring Real Madrid, so it seemed a harsh decision, particularly given the name of his successor.

Romanian Mircea Lucescu was about to undertake his toughest job in Italy. Having only coached Brescia and Reggiana previously – and suffering relegation with both – it was an extremely surprising choice by President Massimo Moratti, and one which left the outgoing boss bemused. In truth, Moratti stated many times afterwards that he'd made a mistake in sacking him; a standpoint he maintained right up until Simoni passed away in the summer of 2020, aged 81.

Whatever the rights and wrongs of it, Simoni's time at the San Siro was up and his successor hardly got off to the most convincing of starts. An injury-time goal from Mikaël Silvestre rescued a point at Vicenza.

Things would soon pick up though. Another late goal – this time from Ronaldo – saw the club pick up three points at Udinese before Roberto Baggio inspired the *nerazzurri* to a 4–1 rout of Roma.

Neighbours Milan were slowly but surely putting together a title challenge following two disastrous seasons. By Christmas they were only a point off the pace following a run of just one defeat in nine matches.

Parma – top of Serie A and scoring goals for fun – looked to have their best-ever chance of becoming Serie A champions. Their lethal striking partnership of Hernán Crespo and Enrico Chiesa meant few

Serie A defences were able to contain them. Over six rounds either side of Christmas Alberto Malesani's side scored an incredible 19 times – including four against Milan, five at Empoli and six at local rivals Piacenza. Unfortunately, the goals dried up towards the end of the campaign and Parma's form suffered as the club had to settle for a fourth-place finish.

Another man making an impressive start was new Milan coach Alberto Zaccheroni. Despite that hammering at Parma they were well in with a shout of landing scudetto number 16. After a tricky start, they lay just a point behind the leaders at Christmas.

Their form was nothing though compared to Lazio, who had recovered from a sluggish start to put together an incredible run of nine straight league wins either side of Christmas. They were scoring freely and it wasn't just their prolific triumvirate of Mancini, Salas and Vieri who were regularly finding the net. Defender Siniša Mihajlović was showing how lethal he was from set pieces, scoring with three free kicks in one game against former club Sampdoria as Lazio romped to a 5–2 win that summed up his former side's plight.

After joining the Genoa club in the summer, coach Luciano Spalletti couldn't arrest his side's chronic run of defeats and after that hammering in Rome he was shown the door. His dismissal came after a desperate run of form which saw Sampdoria hovering just a point above the relegation zone.

Just like at Inter a few weeks before, his replacement was an unexpected one – and it would certainly cause a stir as club President Enrico Mantovani appointed former player and *Gazzetta* star David Platt. Sadly, the appointment was doomed from the outset as the majority of coaches expressed their dissatisfaction with the Englishman being in the dugout when he hadn't even earned his coaching badges.

After seven weeks, the club reappointed Spalletti as the Platt experiment had failed to have the desired effect. Sampdoria wouldn't record a victory under their former midfield star.

Spalletti's former club Empoli were in even worse shape and seemed destined for relegation. A paltry four wins was nowhere near enough – not only that but it'd be a relegation covered in shame as the club were deducted two points in October for allegedly trying to bribe a referee before their 3–0 defeat against Sampdoria.

As we approached the end of 1998, Juventus – despite their decline in form – were just about still in contention, five points adrift of leaders Parma. However, just before Christmas came the bombshell news that coach Marcello Lippi – architect of three scudetti and a Champions League crown during his highly successful tenure – would be joining rivals Inter at the end of the season. As it turned out, his departure from the champions would come much sooner than that.

At the top we had new leaders, as Lazio won their top-of-the-table clash in Parma in a match that will always be remembered for Roberto Mancini's goal of the season; the mercurial forward back-heeling in directly from a corner.

Lazio though weren't stopping there as their incredible sequence of wins showed no sign of ending. Their win in Bari came in a blizzard as the harsh winter conditions reached the far south of the country. There was great concern as to whether we would be having to switch matches at the last minute on *Football Italia*, but thankfully the playing surface at the San Nicola stadium was deemed playable and the match got the go ahead as Lazio recorded a 3–1 victory. The home fans' sole consolation came by way of snowball fights in the stands!

As the season reached the halfway point it was Fiorentina leading the way with Lazio and Parma three points behind. Juventus' title defence was all but over – 11 points off the pace, with Del Piero's season over and French playmaker Zinedine Zidane having an injury-plagued year, it was a pretty miserable winter for the champions.

Marcello Lippi did add a couple of reinforcements though – Juan Esnáider arrived from Espanyol as well as Thierry Henry from Monaco. Both would struggle to settle in Turin though and would leave by the summer ... and within a few weeks Lippi himself was gone too.

A disastrous 4–2 home defeat by Parma (during which the visitors struck three times in six first-half minutes for a first-ever win away to Juventus) meant the end of an era. Shortly after the final whistle in

Turin Lippi walked into the post-match press conference with these words:

> "I have decided to resign. If I am the problem, if the problem is linked to my December announcement about my future [joining Inter], then I'll say good day to you and leave."

Two wins in 13 matches told the story and once the news had broken about Lippi leaving it was only a matter of time. After three scudetti, one Italian Cup, one Champions League trophy as well as a World Club Cup and Intercontinental Cup, this golden era in the club's history was over.

The new man in town was not a popular choice. After gaining a reputation for dull football while at Parma, Carlo Ancelotti had it all to prove in Turin and the fans let the Juventus hierarchy know in no uncertain terms what they thought of the appointment. *"Ancelotti vattene!"* ("Ancelotti, get out!") was the message daubed in graffiti all over Turin, as a legendary coach was being replaced by an unproven one who'd spent his playing career with rivals Milan as well as Roma. Despite the hostility towards him, the new incumbent seemed to resurrect the club's fortunes; Ancelotti's men started to win again.

In the race for the scudetto, Fiorentina had started the New Year in pretty impressive fashion, winning four out of five matches to see them become the new leaders of Serie A. In early February, they hosted Milan, who were looking to cement their place at the top of the table, and it would turn out to be a pivotal afternoon for *Football Italia* viewers – although not for the reasons one might have hoped.

The match saw both sides cancel each other out in a fairly uneventful goalless draw, but with just minutes remaining disaster struck for Giovanni Trapattoni's side. After taking a knock earlier in the second half the *viola* talisman Gabriel Batistuta twisted knee ligaments while chasing a long ball and was immediately stretchered off. The injury didn't turn out to be as serious as first feared but would ultimately cost Fiorentina any chance of winning the title. The Argentine striker would only score three more times in the remaining 14 fixtures.

At the other end of the table an incredible story was playing out. Venezia had experienced a fairly predictable return to the top flight and were just about keeping their heads above water before Álvaro Recoba joined on loan from Inter in what turned out to be one of the signings of the season. With the lethal Uruguayan taking his place up front, Walter Novellino's side went on a sensational run to comfortably survive.

Inspired by the goals of Recoba – who struck ten times in less than half a season with the club – Venezia picked up some notable victories, putting three past both Roma and Inter as well as thrashing Fiorentina 4–1 on the way to finishing in 11th place – an incredible achievement given the club's resources. Novellino would move on to Napoli at the end of the season and guide the southern giants back to Serie A.

In Milan, the clock had seemingly been turned back a few years. The *rossoneri* were flying high, while the *nerazzurri* were in crisis. One defeat in 15 matches had put Alberto Zaccheroni's *rossoneri* right into contention for the title although it still looked like Lazio's to lose – and when the sides shared the points in a goalless draw, the Roman side remained seven points clear. However, there was a sense that Milan's experience and Lazio's lack of it in a scudetto race meant things were far from settled.

Over at Inter a humiliating 4–0 humbling at relegation-bound Sampdoria meant the end for coach Mircea Lucescu. Within a few weeks he was replaced by Roy Hodgson – back for a second spell with the club in a caretaker role before Lippi joined in the summer. He won two of his four matches in charge, the highlight being a thrilling 5–4 win at Roma during which Ronaldo showed flashes of his brilliant best after what had been an injury-plagued season.

A season that started in the Champions League would end without qualification for European football at all, and all the while their city rivals were going from strength to strength.

With seven games to go though, Lazio's seven-point lead had them as odds-on favourites for a first league title in 25 years. However, within a fortnight it was whittled down to just one as Sven-Göran Eriksson's side got the jitters. First – and most painfully – they were ripped apart by bitter rivals Roma in the derby. Even worse, club captain Alessandro Nesta was sent off, meaning he'd be ineligible for the clash with Juventus one week later, where once again everything went wrong.

Even though Christian Vieri twice hit the woodwork, Eriksson's men were left with no one but themselves to blame. Luca Marchegiani's howler in the pouring rain set the tone, as he allowed Henry's shot to beat him at the near post to put Juventus on their way to a 3–1 win in the capital.

The very next day Milan made a statement as coach Zaccheroni and top scorer Oliver Bierhoff returned to Udinese for the first time since joining the *rossoneri* and it would be a triumphant afternoon. Bierhoff scored twice as the *rossoneri* put the home side to the sword in a 5–1 rout. With just a point between Lazio and Milan and five games remaining, the season was reaching a thrilling conclusion. Over the next fortnight Lazio would get their title challenge back on track – indeed both sides would record maximum points to leave the gap intact with just three games left, and that 32nd round of matches looked daunting for Milan.

While Lazio's schedule presented a relatively easy-looking home fixture with Bologna, Milan faced their final really tough hurdle away to Juventus. The *Football Italia* cameras were in Turin for this huge clash between the old rivals. Even though the *bianconeri* had long since given up any chance of making it a hat-trick of scudetti, this was a match that meant everything, regardless of league positions.

After a tense, goalless first half, Milan knew they had a job to do in the second 45 minutes. In the meantime, the production team looked on in horror as the match restarted with our coverage coming from one of the cameras behind the goal.

"WHY THE F*** AREN'T THEY ON CAMERA ONE?!" boomed our director.

"WHY AREN'T THEY F***ING DOING IT?" yelled our producer.

Plenty of industrial language in the gallery and all the while, Milan were attacking towards the far end of the stadium as we looked on. Within 15 seconds George Weah had nodded the visitors ahead and we hardly saw any of it. If you look online you still – to this day –

won't see any main camera coverage of the goal. The millions watching around the world weren't impressed. Safe to say first thing Monday morning an email was fired off to RAI to ask in no uncertain terms what on earth had happened. Weah would later add a second as Milan earned a hugely significant three points but it wouldn't be enough to see them overhaul Lazio, who – as expected – saw off Bologna fairly comfortably.

The following Saturday though – and the penultimate round of the season – would see the race for the scudetto take one potentially decisive twist. While Milan were putting relegated Empoli to the sword at the San Siro, leaders Lazio faced a much tougher task – away to Fiorentina.

After Christian Vieri had cancelled out Gabriel Batistuta's early strike for the *viola*, Lazio knew they had to get a goal or Milan would be going to the final day top of the table. They couldn't break through the *viola* defence though and were actually indebted to keeper Luca Marchegiani for keeping out Rui Costa's second-half penalty.

Now, after 33 matches, Milan had finally moved clear at the top of Serie A and had timed their run to the top spot perfectly. But there was still work to do – a win on the final day was essential, and they were up against a Perugia side still fighting for their place in Serie A. It wouldn't be easy to secure their 16th scudetto in the hostile environment of the Renato Curi stadium.

Milan had won six games in a row with the pressure at its peak at the business end of the season as we headed to the final day. Lazio knew they had to beat Parma and pray for some good news from Perugia – but the first 45 minutes brought quite the reverse. Goals from Guly and Bierhoff had put the *rossoneri* in control at the break.

Lazio would ultimately beat Parma thanks to two goals from Marcelo Salas and with just over ten minutes remaining things got interesting as Perugia pulled one back from the penalty spot. The home side threw everything at the league leaders, who were indebted to the heroics of keeper Christian Abbiati. Perugia couldn't find a way past him though and as the final whistle blew in Umbria the sheer elation on the face of CEO Adriano Galliani said it all.

After a torrid couple of seasons which had seen Milan go from heroes to zeroes, it was a special moment for the club – a resurrection.

Their fans had suffered humiliation after humiliation over the past two seasons – losing to many of the lesser lights of Serie A, as well as going out of the Champions League at home to Norwegian minnows Rosenborg.

The Tabárez experiment had failed. The returns of Sacchi and Capello had been disastrous. So, the club took a chance on one of the country's up-and-coming coaches in Alberto Zaccheroni and had hit the jackpot.

The power of Oliver Bierhoff – who'd come from Udinese with Zaccheroni – had proven crucial. Eighteen goals in his debut season at the San Siro and he'd broken a Serie A record by scoring 15 headed goals throughout the campaign. He had been ably assisted by the ever-reliable George Weah, of course.

As the Champagne flowed in Perugia, the contrast in the capital couldn't have been starker. For Lazio, there was simply abject misery and plenty of tears. The club's long-suffering supporters – so close to only a second title in the club's history – could only watch on and wonder what might have been. They did have the consolation though of a first Champions League campaign. Once again, the northern powerhouses of Milan and Turin had maintained their stranglehold on the scudetto.

As the *tifosi* were filing out of the Stadio Olimpico the feeling was that Lazio had blown the best chance they'd have of claiming a second scudetto. Seven points ahead of Milan at one stage, that advantage was all but frittered away by two pivotal defeats in a week at the Stadio Olimpico against Roma and Juventus. While they just about kept ahead of Milan over the ensuing weeks, Sven-Göran Eriksson's men were unable to match the *rossoneri*'s relentless run of wins and after they were held in Florence on the penultimate weekend of the season the game was up. Little did the club's fans know then what lay ahead.

7

ETERNAL JOY – PART ONE

While the end of May brought joy to Milan, there were plenty of other winners and losers in Serie A. Parma added to the two European trophies they'd previously won. After thrashing Marseille 3–0 in the UEFA Cup Final in Moscow, Italy could now boast six titles for its clubs in that competition during the decade, maintaining its status at the top of European football.

In Genoa though there were tears as Sampdoria – just eight years on from their being crowned champions of Italy – were relegated from Serie A as their near 20-year stay in Italy's top flight came to an end. The city wouldn't be represented in Serie A at all in the 1999/2000 campaign following city rivals Genoa's mediocre Serie B campaign.

Another big name was back though, as Torino returned to the top flight after three seasons away. A fine Serie B campaign had seen them join Verona and the southern pair of Reggina and Lecce in the top flight. While Verona and Lecce had spent many years fluctuating between Serie A and B it was a fairytale for Reggina, as it would be their debut season at the pinnacle of Italian football. Situated deep in the south in the town of Reggio Calabria (more famous for its ferry to Sicily than its football team) they'd finally earned their place among the cream of *calcio*. The journey wouldn't end there though as they'd go on to surprise all of Serie A's big guns – taking points off the lot of them.

At the other end of the footballing spectrum (and indeed the country) stood Italy's most successful club – Juventus. While Torino were celebrating being back among the big boys, it was a summer of bitter recriminations for Juventus, following their worst campaign in almost a decade. It resulted in the club having to compete in the much-maligned Intertoto Cup – Juve's only hope of securing European football over the coming campaign. That meant their season starting in July – something the club would live to regret, as not only did it mean a ten-month slog, but also an early exit in the UEFA Cup – rendering that decision foolhardy as things turned out.

Going into his first full campaign with the club, coach Carlo Ancelotti had made changes. After eight hugely successful seasons in Turin, experienced keeper Angelo Peruzzi was off to join the Lippi revolution at Inter. His replacement was Edwin van der Sar who'd won it all with Ajax and had been a mainstay of his national team for some years. He joined on a free transfer after his contract expired with the Dutch giants and was joined in Turin by defender Gianluca Zambrotta – signed from Bari for £7 million. The 22-year-old was very well thought of following two excellent seasons with the southern club. While these two additions were the main business Juventus would conduct in the summer of 1999, over at Inter there were changes of epic proportions.

As had been revealed six months earlier, Marcello Lippi was the latest man entrusted to deliver Inter's first scudetto in a decade and the squad was significantly strengthened over the summer. Christian Vieri led the way – arriving from Lazio for a world record fee of £28 million. Christian Panucci was signed from Real Madrid to bolster the defence while Clarence Seedorf also made the move from the Spanish capital.

Milan were also busy – and they brought in a player who'd go on to become a *rossoneri* legend. Andriy Shevchenko was snapped up from Dynamo Kiev for a fee in excess of £20 million, as the champions strengthened what was already a ruthless machine.

Down in the capital there were big changes too. After being relegated it was always highly unlikely that Sampdoria would be able to hold on to star striker Vincenzo Montella and so it proved, as he headed south to Roma – also entering a new era under Fabio Capello.

Across town at Lazio Sven-Göran Eriksson needed to find a way to replace Christian Vieri. With new signings Simone Inzaghi and

Fabrizio Ravanelli joining other offensive options such as Salas, Bokšić and Mancini, it seemed the previous season's runners-up had plenty of options in attack.

So, to the big kick-off and the champions made the long trip south to newly promoted Lecce. Despite a debut goal for Shevchenko, the *rossoneri* were forced to settle for a disappointing 2–2 draw as their opponents twice came from behind to rescue a point.

Juventus didn't fare much better either against new boys Reggina (not to be confused with former Serie A side Reggiana) as the minnows earned a famous point in Turin, thanks to Mohamed Kallon's second-half header.

Inter hosted another newly promoted side at the San Siro and made a statement to their rivals, thrashing Verona 3–0 with debutant Christian Vieri grabbing a hat-trick. It was the perfect start to their new era. They would go on to pick up ten points from the first five games with star signing Vieri on fire, his stunning strike in the 5–1 rout of Parma proving to be one of the goals of the season.

The others were doing their best to keep up. Lazio started their title challenge impressively, while Milan were scoring goals for fun. No fewer than 14 came in the first five games as new signing Andriy Shevchenko made a great start to life at the San Siro. His hat-trick at the Stadio Olimpico – where Milan shared eight goals with Lazio in one of the games of the season – was a sign of things to come for the Ukrainian.

Juventus though had a fairly indifferent start. Defeat at Lecce left the *bianconeri* fans far from impressed as performances showed little sign of improving even with Alessandro Del Piero back from injury. His long absence understandably had a huge effect on him when he was back playing – he would struggle for goals throughout the campaign.

In mid-October Juventus finally showed their title credentials, winning 1–0 at Roma thanks to an exquisite free kick from Zinedine Zidane. Carlo Ancelotti's side were seemingly beginning to click into gear.

The surprise package was Serie A-debutant side Reggina, who didn't taste defeat until week five. Incredibly they would find themselves joint second in the season's early stages to leave their fans in dreamland.

By late October the derbies were starting to come thick and fast – and the first of those came at the San Siro. Inter went into it three points ahead of their rivals – despite their unbeaten run surprisingly ending the previous week at struggling Venezia. In front of a capacity crowd the *Football Italia* cameras made a rare Saturday-night appearance – and it'd be a night full of drama and controversy.

After firing Inter ahead from the penalty spot, Ronaldo was about to hit the headlines for the wrong reasons, as an alleged elbow offence on Milan's Roberto Ayala resulted in a first red card in Serie A for Inter's Brazilian star.

Despite the one-goal advantage, Marcello Lippi's side still had to survive an hour with ten men. By the time Andriy Shevchenko finally equalised, Inter had 17 minutes to see out. When their opponents were reduced to ten men too, following Ayala's red card late on, it seemed it'd finish honours even. However, a 90th-minute header from George Weah broke *nerazzurri* hearts as Milan stole it at the death.

A fortnight later the sequence of derbies headed to Turin for *"il Derby della Mole"*. The two sides hadn't faced each other in three years following Torino's relegation to Serie B in 1996 and this hotly anticipated fixture attracted a bumper attendance of 60,000 to the Stadio delle Alpi.

However, the match would prove to be something of an anti-climax. Juventus failed to get any sort of momentum and, with their opponents looking to frustrate the *bianconeri* at every turn, it would end goalless. It was a result that would leave Carlo Ancelotti's men three points behind Lazio, who had swept to the top of the table following an unbeaten start to the season. A fortnight later though – in the next round of matches – that would change dramatically.

The live game on Channel 4 was the Rome derby and while the *Football Italia* viewers were able to watch the live action from the Stadio Olimpico, the production team had also been busy working hard behind the scenes for a unique feature on the fixture for our *Gazzetta* viewers the following Saturday.

As regular viewers would have seen on a weekly basis, pre-match choreography in Italian stadia is a huge part of the *calcio* matchday experience, especially in the biggest games – the derbies, whenever the big guns come to town as well as any of Juventus, Milan or Inter meet. The roar when the teams come out – which is such a big thing over here in the UK – is often outshone by the thrilling and colourful spectacle of flags, scarves, flares and smoke that precede many a match in Italy – and it is rarely more impressive than in the Stadio Olimpico when Roma and Lazio face off.

So ahead of the final *derby della capitale* of the millennium the *Gazzetta* crew went undercover to the Lazio hardcore ultras' headquarters just outside Rome to see what they had planned for the forthcoming showdown with Roma. We got to see how they plan for these games to the finest detail. Their mission – to outdo their rivals – is something seen as very much a way of showing their allegiance to their club in the most loyal way they can. They are the most passionate fans of all, who travel the length and breadth of Italy every week.

We had managed to negotiate a way of filming the choreography display in the Curva Nord – the traditional home end of the Stadio Olimpico for Lazio's hardcore fans – and pre-match the stadium is a sight to behold with one end of this massive arena blue and the other end red.

As for the game, our crew filming it were obviously desperate for a Lazio win given the passion and intensity this fixture creates, but they were to be devastated as Sven-Göran Eriksson's side were blown away in the first half in one of the most one-sided Rome derbies for years. Two goals apiece from star signing Vincenzo Montella as well as Marco Delvecchio had the *giallorossi* in dreamland at the break. Siniša Mihajlović's second-half penalty wasn't even a consolation as things turned hostile in the Curva Nord, meaning the *Gazzetta* crew had to make a run for it!

While Lazio were floundering, Juventus were about to make a statement, taking full advantage of Lazio's disastrous derby showing to draw level with Eriksson's men at the top of the table. Just six months on from their home defeat to Milan, this match couldn't have been a greater contrast. The *bianconeri* were about to gain revenge, cruising past the reigning champions 3–1.

With the team back at the top of Serie A, things finally seemed like they were returning to normal for Juventus after a turbulent 1999, which had seen the emotional departure of Marcello Lippi. Finally it appeared the fans were finally beginning to warm to Carlo Ancelotti – the biggest plus for him being the return to the side of Alessandro Del Piero.

After his horrific knee injury some twelve months earlier the *bianconeri* star was back in the starting line-up. While he was struggling for goals – his two so far coming from the penalty spot – he was instrumental against Milan, setting up two for Antonio Conte and Filippo Inzaghi.

Next up for the *bianconeri* and Del Piero was a trip to a Lazio side still reeling from their derby humiliation. The top-of-the-table clash turned out to be a bit of anti-climax as the two sides had to settle for a point apiece after a goalless draw. All of a sudden though there were three teams level at the top of Serie A – Juventus, Lazio and now their city rivals Roma.

That derby win for the *giallorossi* was just one of four consecutive league victories as they were right in the scudetto hunt under the leadership of new boss – four-time title winner Fabio Capello. Unfortunately, their winning run would soon come to an end, a 1–0 defeat at Bologna the prelude to a sequence of one win in four games which would see the side from the capital fall off the pace. Their title campaign had been blown off course and they wouldn't recover.

As for Juventus, the big matches kept on coming. After the gruelling Turin derby, they had faced Milan and Lazio in consecutive weeks and now Inter were coming to town. There was only one thing on everyone's mind though – Marcello Lippi's return to the Stadio delle Alpi after his dramatic departure in February. This would be the first time he'd face Juventus here since bringing his Napoli side to Turin some six years earlier.

There were several other reunions too. Angelo Peruzzi faced his former employers after joining Inter in the summer. In addition to their keeper, Christian Vieri, Vladimir Jugović and substitute Roberto

Baggio all returned to their old stomping ground for this hugely anticipated fixture.

Lippi's side had enjoyed a revival in the build-up to this huge clash, winning their last three games and in the process scoring ten times and not conceding at all. The *nerazzurri* went into the match also knowing a win would send them above their opponents. Defeat though, would mean they'd be five points behind Juventus. It was a crucial clash in the build-up to Christmas.

Once again the match was shrouded in controversy. Some 20 months on from Mark Iuliano's barge on Ronaldo that was so pivotal in the title race, the referee was once again at the centre of attention.

Following a mistake from Paolo Montero, Inter striker Iván Zamorano was clean through on goal and after being taken out on the edge of the box the visitors were incensed not once but twice. First, their penalty shouts fell on deaf ears as Daniele Tombolini awarded a free kick on the edge of the box before only giving Juventus keeper Edwin van der Sar a yellow card.

To add insult to injury, the *bianconeri* would soon go one up as Alessandro Del Piero crossed for Filippo Inzaghi to sweep home his seventh goal of the season. Van der Sar would eventually see red in the second half following a handball outside the area, but Inter couldn't make the most of their numerical advantage as they ended the evening five points behind their bitter rivals.

Things would get even worse for Marcello Lippi's side the following week as 1999 ended on a sour note. A 2–1 loss at the San Nicola stadium to Bari made it an incredible five straight defeats in five meetings with the southern club on what was a famous night for the home team. Prior to this run of victories, they'd only beaten their more illustrious opponents six times in their entire history!

Hugo Enyinnaya set the hosts on their way with an absolute rocket from all of 40 yards into the top corner and although Inter swiftly equalised through Christian Vieri, it'd be a local boy who'd eventually take centre stage.

Substitute Antonio Cassano, just 17 years old and making his home debut in what was only a second career appearance, was Bari born and bred. He'd grown up in the old part of the port city (Bari Vecchia) where there was very little money to speak of. His dream was to become a footballer and from a young age he'd always be seen kicking a ball about on the streets of the southern city. After being spotted by a scout from Bari he worked his way through the club's youth system before finally getting his breakthrough in the 1999/2000 season.

He'd made his debut against Puglian rivals Lecce a week before the big match with Inter. With the score still locked at 1–1 against the *nerazzurri* and the game heading towards the 90th minute, Cassano chose the perfect moment to announce himself on the big stage. Controlling a long ball forward with his heel before turning the Inter defence inside out, he coolly despatched the ball past Fabrizio Ferron in the Inter goal, and headed off to the Curva Nord to celebrate raucously with the Bari ultras. Besieged by reporters after the game, it'd be the goal that would launch a career spent among the leading lights both at home and abroad – featuring the likes of Roma, Real Madrid, Milan as well as Inter themselves.

As Bari were celebrating there were recriminations at Inter. A season that started so well was now beginning to fall apart and with the gap between themselves and the top increasing week by week it was a fairly miserable Christmas.

While Inter were struggling, it'd be Lazio though who would go into the New Year with a two-point lead at the top following victory over Piacenza, as Juventus were held to a 1–1 draw at Fiorentina. We looked set for a thrilling title race as we moved into the new millennium. It didn't disappoint.

Lazio's New Year started in disastrous fashion though as they were sunk 2–0 at Venezia – and Juventus took full advantage. Pippo Inzaghi picked up from where he had left off before Christmas, scoring the only goal against Verona to put the Turin giants a point clear at the Serie A summit.

Meantime, while Lazio were fighting it out for the title with Juventus, across town at Roma things weren't going brilliantly either on or off the pitch. While they were in a respectable third place, they were five points behind Lazio following a dip in form resulting in losses to both Bologna and Parma. That, though, was just the tip of the iceberg, as off the field they were allegedly involved in one of the season's big scandals.

A report in the press emerged of Roma gifting Rolex watches to the tune of £8,000 to two match officials as a "Christmas present". The counter argument: "AS Roma notes that the gifts had a lower value than those sent by other clubs." As it transpired, Inter were also revealed to have given each referee a muscle exerciser worth £500, but rumours swept the league of more lavish presents from other clubs.

La Gazzetta dello Sport claimed that Roma had given Rolex watches to 37 referees. Luciano Nizzola – President of the Italian Football Federation – said officials should return gifts "that cannot be considered normal gifts that accompany the end of year festivities". The Federation were unimpressed at Roma's claim of buying a bulk batch of Rolexes at a discount. As the *Corriere della Sera* put it: "better to be stingy than corrupt".

As the season reached the halfway mark it was Juventus who were crowned "winter champions" following a 3–0 win over Perugia. It was a victory that was sealed with a goal from striker Darko Kovačevič. He was earning a "super-sub" tag in Turin. Despite not getting much of a look in with Juve's starting XI, he was chipping in with a few useful goals following his arrival from Real Sociedad the previous summer.

Kovačević would score again the next week as Juventus won 2–0 at Reggina on a day that the gap at the top would extend to three points following Lazio's goalless draw at Cagliari. However, the *bianconeri* would soon drop points too. The following week it was their turn to be left frustrated by the Sardinians following a surprising 1–1 draw in Turin.

Six days later they dropped more points – this time at Udinese – as Alessandro Del Piero returned to the ground where he'd suffered his horrific knee injury just 15 months earlier. Just like in that fixture the match would end in a draw. Juventus were actually indebted to the unlikely figure of Ciro Ferrara, who rescued a point for them.

By now Lazio had reclaimed the Serie A leadership but the side from the capital were about to hit choppy waters themselves. A disappointing home draw with Parma followed by defeat at Milan left them trailing Juventus by four points following their 4–0 win at relegation-bound Venezia. However, post-match the conversation was not about the *bianconieri*'s thumping win but the ever-deteriorating relationship between the front two – Filippo Inzaghi and Alessandro Del Piero.

After his horror injury which had wiped out three-quarters of Juve's disastrous 1998/99 campaign, the number ten had thankfully enjoyed an injury-free season thus far but things were still far from perfect. All of his five goals so far had come from the penalty spot, whereas Inzaghi had scored 12 times. Del Piero had assisted over half of these and things came to a head after the final whistle in Venice.

With Del Piero scoring his goal from the penalty spot it was Inzaghi once again who took centre stage, scoring a hat-trick late on in the game. However, all three of his second-half goals could have been claimed by his strike partner and on two of them he all but took the ball off Del Piero's feet as he was shaping up to score from close range. The other goal could have seen him lay the ball off to the number ten who was in oceans of space, but Inzaghi chose to go it alone, scoring at the second attempt.

Del Piero did his best to hide his anger. After a tough first year back from injury he felt his strike partner was being selfish. A couple of goals in the game would have kept the press quiet and would bring an end to the unwanted statistic of him not scoring from open play since coming back into the side at the start of the season.

His anger was pretty clear in his post-match interviews, stating Inzaghi was "lucky to score" and also that he decided against passing to his team mate "unless the moment was right". While they remained professional on the field their relationship off it never recovered and just over a year later Inzaghi would leave Juventus.

Despite the falling out of their attacking partnership, the wins just kept on coming. Roma, Bari and Piacenza were all seen off, meaning Carlo Ancelotti's side had claimed five successive victories and over the same period Lazio had dropped seven points. The gap at the top was ever-growing as we headed into another huge weekend, which many thought had already ended the scudetto race.

Juventus met Torino in the second *Derby della Mole* of the season, where it wasn't just the *bianconeri* who needed the points. In their first season back in Serie A the *granata* were struggling with their heads just below water in the relegation zone.

After a goalless and uneventful first derby back in November this meeting couldn't have been more contrasting. The old adage about the team at the bottom having no luck certainly rang true in this match.

Midway through the first half Alessio Tacchinardi's long-range shot took a freakish deflection off Massimo Brambilla to sail over the hapless Luca Bucci and put Juventus one up.

Torino fought back though and before long Marco Ferrante had squared things up from the penalty spot. The Roman forward was enjoying quite a prolific spell – this was the 13th goal of the season in what was by far and away the most productive one of his career.

It stayed level until just past the hour mark, when Ciro Ferrara chose the perfect moment to score only his second goal of the season. The win looked secure when Alessandro Del Piero made it 3–1 from the spot soon after and although Ferrante converted what was remarkably the third penalty of the match late on it remained 3–2 as Juventus celebrated a sixth straight win.

Some 300 kilometres to the east – at the Marcantonio Bentegodi stadium in Verona – Lazio were doing their best to keep in touch with the league leaders. Unfortunately for the side from the capital they were about to suffer a quite disastrous afternoon.

As if going down to a 1–0 defeat and losing yet more ground on Juventus wasn't bad enough, they were about to lose two key men for the Rome derby, which was just seven days away. First set-piece specialist Siniša Mihajlović picked up a yellow card which would result in a ban for the Roma match. Then – and far more damagingly – club captain Alessandro Nesta went off injured. He'd go on to be missing for the derby too.

The gap at the top was now nine points – bigger than it had been all season. Juventus were unbeaten in an incredible 22 matches, yet they still looked to have two tricky hurdles to overcome over the next couple of weeks; away to Milan and at home to their closest challengers – Lazio.

The match at the San Siro was brought forward to Friday evening, meaning it was going to be another late night *Gazzetta* edit as we had highlights of this huge clash to put into the show.

"You've got five minutes for this edit, maximum five and a half. Don't go over that. We'll be in the pub!" were the words from my boss as I went up to the third floor of our facilities house to watch the match. The rest of the show was edited so it was seen as a drinking opportunity – where else would you spend a couple of spare hours on a Friday night?

As it turned out it was to prove a hugely significant night in the title race. Milan's 2–0 win brought Juve's long unbeaten run to an end thanks to two goals from star signing Andriy Shevchenko, but the match could have been so different as Filippo Inzaghi wasted the chance of the match in the first half while the match was still goalless.

Having intercepted an uncharacteristically sloppy pass from Paolo Maldini, the Juventus forward was clear on goal and after rounding Christian Abbiati he somehow fired wide of an open goal. It'd prove to be a huge miss in the context of the race for the scudetto, as Shevchenko made the league leaders pay the ultimate price.

Suddenly Lazio saw an opening, but to get back into the title race they simply had to win the derby. They knew a victory here would mean a six-point gap heading to what was becoming an eagerly awaited scudetto showdown seven days later in Turin.

Not only that, they wanted revenge for their derby disaster back in November when Roma had scored four times in the first half. They hadn't reckoned though on another disastrous start. Vincenzo Montella – one of their tormentors in chief back in November – put the *giallorossi* ahead inside two minutes. This time though it'd be a false dawn. Pavel Nedvěd poked home an equaliser before Juan Sebastian Verón's exquisite free kick put Lazio ahead. It'd prove to be the winner, and Lazio would be heading to Turin with the gap reduced to six points. A win at the Stadio delle Alpi would set the cat among the pigeons.

A few weeks earlier I'd requested the weekend of 1 and 2 April off work; thankfully it had been granted, as I'd concocted a plan to go to the potential scudetto decider – as ever though the itinerary was a complicated one! It involved flying to Geneva, hiring a car, picking up a friend who was studying at university there and then driving through Switzerland, France and Italy to get to Turin.

Due to our connections with RAI (the Italian state broadcasters) I'd managed to negotiate a couple of press pass tickets. The anticipation of this match was huge. Everywhere you looked – television, newspapers, internet – all anyone was talking about was this clash that would potentially decide the scudetto.

The general consensus was that a win for Juventus and it was theirs, whereas a Lazio win meant anything was possible. The atmosphere was electric inside the Stadio delle Alpi on this warm spring evening. All inside this vast arena knew that there was 90 minutes of tension ahead.

As expected it was an incredibly cagey game. Chances were at a premium. You got the impression that the longer it stayed goalless, the happier Juventus would be. Keep the six-point cushion intact with six games left and they were in the box seat for the title.

Then, on 65 minutes, there was huge drama as Ciro Ferrara received a second yellow card after hauling back Simone Inzaghi. It really was time now for Juventus to batten down the hatches – to come out of this match with a draw would surely be a big psychological advantage.

Within two minutes there was a goal. To Lazio. Diego Simeone's precise header stunned the home fans and try as they might the ten men couldn't find a way past Marco Ballotta. As the final whistle sounded to almost stunned silence, Juve's lead had shrunk from nine points to three in just a fortnight. The race for the scudetto was on.

An hour later I arrived back at my hotel. The concierge (a big Juventus fan) said to me "the league has gone now, Juventus won't win it. They're exhausted, their season started in July in the Intertoto Cup." He was right in one regard – Juventus were tired. Unbeaten in 22 matches, they'd now suffered back-to-back defeats – the second of which was potentially disastrous.

The following weekend saw the gap go perilously close to just one point as Juventus looked like being frustrated by Bologna. Chance after chance went begging before Darko Kovačević headed home in the 89th minute. Massimo Paganin's own goal rubbed salt in Bologna's wounds as Carlo Ancelotti breathed a huge sigh of relief.

The following week saw yet another twist in this incredible title race as what looked to be a one-point gap during Juve's game with Bologna a week earlier became five. The *bianconeri*'s bitter rivals Fiorentina (and former coach Giovanni Trapattoni) did them a massive favour as Gabriel Batistuta's injury-time free kick denied Lazio victory in a six-goal thriller.

Juventus were at the San Siro later on that day to face an Inter side that had long given up on the title, lying as they were some 13 points behind the leaders. For the second straight week, it was Kovačević who proved the hero – striking twice in the second half as Juventus recorded a 2–1 victory.

After the top two both posted wins the following week, the title race was blown wide open with two matches to go. While Lazio edged a five-goal thriller with Venezia, Juventus were about to suffer a third defeat in six games as Verona – who'd seen off Lazio six weeks earlier – put Juventus to the sword, cruising to a 2–0 win.

Cesare Prandelli's side had taken Serie A by surprise on their return to the top flight and would finish the season in the top half. Top scorer Fabrizio Cammarata struck both goals as the gap at the top was reduced to two points with just two games left. And if the last month or so had been eventful, we hadn't seen anything yet. The final fortnight of the campaign would be full of drama, controversy and tears – of joy and ecstasy.

Juventus went into their final home game against Parma aware that a win over coach Carlo Ancelotti's former side could be enough for the title. Lazio travelled to Bologna knowing anything other than a win and their title dream could be over.

Despite two goals from former Lazio idol Beppe Signori, Sven-Göran Eriksson's men edged another five-goal thriller, but the real drama was in Turin. After Alessandro Del Piero had finally scored from open play (for the first time in some 567 days), Juventus looked set to keep the two-point gap intact.

In added time though, there was a hugely controversial moment that would rival the Ronaldo penalty incident from two years earlier.

Future Juventus star Fabio Cannavaro headed in from a corner only for referee Massimo De Santis to rule it out for a foul. It seemed a harsh call and many around the country were pointing out that, just like with the Ronaldo episode, Juventus were benefiting from some dubious refereeing decisions in big games.

Whether it was the right or the wrong call was now immaterial. We were heading to the final day of the season with the scudetto on the line. Not only that but we were heading to Perugia once again to see it play out.

While Milan had glorious memories of their title win at the Renato Curi stadium 12 months earlier, Juve's previous last-day experience in Umbria had brought nothing but pain.

On the final day of the 1975/76 season a 1–0 defeat to Perugia thanks to a goal from Renato Curi (the man after whom the stadium is named) meant the *bianconeri* missed out on the title and worse still, bitter rivals Torino won it.

Unlike the previous year when Milan won the title in Perugia, the home side were safe from relegation and even though Lazio had a home banker against another team who'd avoided relegation – Reggina – nobody thought Juventus' two-point advantage could be overturned on the final day of the season. It turned into one of the most dramatic afternoons in Serie A history.

It all started as expected. Shot after shot rained in on the Perugia goal but Juventus couldn't convert their superiority into goals and the first half ended goalless. Meanwhile, 170 kilometres south in Rome, Lazio were having few difficulties. Two first-half penalties (from Simone Inzaghi and Juan Sebastián Verón) had them two up at the interval and in cruise control.

Then it started to rain in Perugia; slowly at first. Before long it turned into a thunderstorm and the second half was delayed. As the two matches were supposed to be played at exactly the same time, Lazio's clash with Reggina was also halted, under glorious summer skies.

While James Richardson and his guests were chatting during the extended half-time break our coverage would intermittently head across to the Stadio Olimpico too, where there was all sorts of confusion. The match officials didn't want to restart the match until the Perugia versus Juventus clash had resumed as the two fixtures had to be played in tandem.

The rain had now turned into a storm of biblical proportions at the Renato Curi stadium. The pitch was underwater, fans were leaving in their droves and in the meantime the league title was on the line! Referee Pierluigi Collina would come out intermittently to see if the ball would bounce – which seemed utterly futile. The ball wouldn't travel and given the situation the decision was made to restart the Lazio versus Reggina game.

Diego Simeone would add a third goal as Lazio cruised to victory, meaning they had a one-point lead with 45 minutes left to play in Perugia. Therefore, a draw for Juventus would mean a play-off with Lazio for the title and a win would see them over the line. A defeat didn't bear thinking about.

After a break of well over an hour it was decided the match would finish and even though the rain had stopped the conditions were far from perfect. Every challenge would see surface water spray in all directions and on 50 minutes the unthinkable happened – defender Alessandro Calori capitalised on a loose ball to fire his side ahead.

"That's set the cat among the pigeons!" boomed Peter Brackley on *Football Italia*. It was a goal that sent the Stadio Olimpico faithful into delirium while in Perugia the Juventus players, staff and fans were shell-shocked. Juventus had 40 minutes to score the goal that would at least give them the chance of a play-off for the title and they poured forward at every opportunity, but keeping the ball under control was proving difficult. Filippo Inzaghi failed to get on the end of a Del Piero cross as the ball skidded across the face of goal. When Juventus did manage to get a strike on target, they found keeper Andrea Mazzantini an impenetrable barrier in the Perugia goal.

When the *bianconeri* lost Gianluca Zambrotta to a second yellow card late on, the game was up for Juventus as their title campaign ended in controversy and devastation.

Down in the capital though there were tears of joy as Lazio claimed what was only their second scudetto and in their centenary year too. "I never thought it would be this beautiful," beamed coach

Sven-Göran Eriksson. "The other titles I won elsewhere in Europe cannot compare to this."

After coming from nine points behind in mid-March it was an incredible triumph against all the odds, but where had it all gone wrong for Juventus? The real problem was goals – or the lack of them. With Del Piero far from back to his best following injury, the *bianconeri* scored just 46 times in the entire campaign. Despite their watertight defence, the lack of firepower was the story of their crushing afternoon in Umbria. Only Verona in the top half had scored fewer goals.

In the final analysis though the most damaging defeat perhaps wasn't the one against Lazio in April, even though it seemed so at the time. Juve's defeat in Verona three games from the end was hugely significant – a win there would have given them a five-point lead with two games to play. The defeat at the Bentegodi stadium left Carlo Ancelotti's side with precious little margin for error. The scars left in Perugia would take a long time to heal and the ultimate irony was that Carlo Mazzone – a passionate, lifelong Roma fan – was the coach who handed the title to the *giallorossi*'s greatest enemy.

There was misery on the other side of town too as Torino's return to the top flight would only be a fleeting one. Cagliari, Venezia and Piacenza joined the *granata* in Serie B and before the season was done there were yet more tears to come.

They came in the first leg of the Coppa Italia Final between Lazio and Inter. The *nerazzurri*'s Brazilian superstar – Ronaldo – was making his comeback off the bench after five months out due to having ruptured a tendon in his knee.

Six minutes into his return disaster struck. The Brazilian attempted a stepover and he collapsed to the turf in agony. This injury proved to be even more serious than the previous one, as he had completely torn his kneecap tendon. As he left the field to a standing ovation – screaming with agony on a stretcher – there were doubts he'd ever be able to play again. As it turned out he wouldn't return for over a year.

As the Italian season drew to a close, Lazio added the Coppa Italia to their scudetto to make it a domestic double after an unforgettable season. The scudetto had returned to the capital for the first time since 1983 – the question was, could it stay there?

8

ETERNAL JOY – PART TWO

It was a glorious midsummer's day and I was minding my own business in the *Football Italia* office as I tended to do during the off season, trying to make myself look busy even though I had absolutely nothing to do. My boss walked over.

"Myself and Jim [the Production Manager] have something we need to talk to you about. Do you have any plans for lunch?"

"Er, no." I replied.

"Right. We'll swing by at one o clock. See you in a bit."

I had no idea what they were up to. It was going to be a long summer as it was as the Sydney Olympics weren't scheduled to finish until the end of September, meaning that the Serie A kick-off wouldn't be until the start of October. I would have to try to look busy for quite some time. Just as well that the European Championships were about to start.

"Right, let's go. Time for lunch."

Off we went to a café in a North London high street and, little did I realise, my working life was about to be turned upside down.

"Channel 4 have to make a certain percentage of their programmes regional productions, so we won't be able to operate out of London any more. We've had a look at potential facilities and have decided to move up to Leeds, with our production coming out of Yorkshire Television."

It was a bolt from the blue. I was told that if I wanted to carry on working on the show it wouldn't be feasible for me to stay in London.

I had to move to Leeds. They'd sort out accommodation for me, but I would soon be heading to Yorkshire.

The move north was absolutely fine personally. I found a nice little flat for myself and my girlfriend (who'd selflessly made the decision to leave her job in London to move with me) and we settled in really nicely.

Our offices were actually in Sheffield which meant a 45-minute commute each day. The only major problem was the logistics of moving our entire tape library up north. This consisted of eight years or so of broadcasting our show, which roughly equated to about 5,000 tapes that had to make their way up the M1 so they could be stored at Yorkshire TV.

There were also many changes to our editing as finally we would be embracing the new age of television by no longer editing on tape. We were about to break new ground by editing on Avid. For the traditionalists amongst us editing in this new tapeless way seemed a step into the unknown.

All our archive and match recordings would still be recorded on tape, which would mean a lot of the footage we needed would have to be transferred into the Avid to edit. So, when we came to edit *Gazzetta*, all the tapes with James' links and interviews that had been brought back from Italy that week would have to be played into the Avid, which was the best part of two hours gone before we could start editing the show! These were big changes compared to what we'd all been used to and we had a few teething troubles. Nevertheless, within a few weeks the well-oiled machine that the production was had overcome any logistical issues.

Still, there was plenty of time to get prepared for the new Serie A season, which, as already mentioned, was delayed to accommodate the Olympics. There were some major changes afoot all round Italy's top flight before the new campaign finally got underway.

One of the big stories was Napoli's return to the limelight. After a couple of seasons away we had the two-time Serie A winners back and after a lean few years it was great to see the south of Italy have more representation at the highest level. They'd be joining Reggina, Bari and Lecce to give the league a very different flavour for the

2000/01 campaign. Promoted alongside Napoli were Serie B champions Vicenza as well as bitter local rivals Brescia and Atalanta.

On the field, there were big changes of personnel ahead of the new season and the biggest spenders were Roma. Following bitter rivals Lazio's incredible scudetto triumph they needed to make a statement and they couldn't have made a bigger one as in came one of the most explosive strikers in world football. Gabriel Batistuta ended a nine-year association with Fiorentina, signing for Roma in a transfer worth well in excess of £30 million.

The Argentinian striker wasn't the only South American to link up with the *giallorossi* though. Defender Walter Samuel joined from Boca Juniors for just under £20 million along with Brazilian midfielder Emerson – snapped up from Bayer Leverkusen for £16 million.

Roma also forked out the best part of £20 million snapping up Japanese international Hidetoshi Nakata from Perugia. Under multiple title-winner Fabio Capello, they meant business.

The big-spending champions had a statement of their own to make, breaking the world transfer record to sign Hernán Crespo from Parma for £35 million. He'd join fellow South Americans Marcelo Salas and Claudio López in attack.

Juventus were desperate to bolster their attacking options and identified the man to fire them to the scudetto. David Trezeguet had broken Italian hearts that summer, scoring twice in the Euro 2000 Final as France were crowned European champions. He moved to Turin from Monaco for £20 million.

There were yet more changes at Inter too. With Ronaldo's season a write-off and Christian Vieri being frustrated by injury, some replacements were needed up front with Álvaro Recoba and Iván Zamorano the only recognised names. Their choices were surprising to say the least. Step forward Turkish international Hakan Şükür and even more surprisingly Robbie Keane from Coventry City. Neither would set the world on fire at the San Siro and Keane would only make six appearances before joining Leeds United in a loan agreement, which was made permanent the following summer.

Inter also bade farewell to Roberto Baggio. He left at the end of his contract to join newly promoted Brescia, following his falling-out with coach Marcello Lippi. It was a major scoop for the Lombardy club who were no doubt hoping he could repeat the magic he had created at Bologna three years earlier, when he scored 22 goals in a season – gaining a call-up to the national side for the 1998 World Cup.

The *Football Italia* season kicked off in the capital as big-spending Roma enjoyed a routine win over Bologna, thanks to Francesco Totti and a Marcello Castellini own goal. The real story on the opening day though was happening 700 kilometres south, deep into Calabria, as Inter's season was about to get off to a shocking start – at Reggina.

Despite an early goal from Álvaro Recoba, the home side fought back and goals either side of half time from Davide Possanzini and Massimo Marazzina saw the *nerazzurri* get off to the worst possible start – but that wasn't the big story of the day: the very same evening Marcello Lippi was sacked.

This defeat followed a disastrous start to the campaign which had seen them knocked out of the Champions League in the qualifying rounds by Swedish minnows Helsingborgs. Post-match Marcello Lippi made a short statement before walking out, claiming the team played like "spoiled children". He continued, "they think they are great players and the victories will arrive. That is not fair to those who pay them or not to those who go to watch them. Today if I was the President I would dismiss the coach and line the players up against a wall and give them all a kick up the backside."

In stepped Marco Tardelli, a former player for the *nerazzurri* who, since becoming a coach, had impressed – guiding the Italian Under-21 side to European Championship glory.

Juventus, meanwhile, kicked off their season with the events in Perugia some four and a half months earlier still in their minds and their title challenge got underway at newly promoted Napoli. In front of their passionate, raucous crowd, the home side started impressively. Roberto Stellone's goal shortly before half time gave their season lift-off to the delight of almost all of the 70,000 inside the San Paolo stadium.

Juventus though would show their class to turn the match on its head. Darko Kovačević headed the *bianconeri* level before Alessandro

Del Piero curled home a trademark right-footed effort to get the Turin giants off to the perfect start.

In fact, none of the promoted sides won on the opening weekend, although Atalanta did hold champions Lazio to a 2–2 draw in Bergamo. Brescia went down 4–2 at Udinese while Serie B champions Vicenza lost 2–0 at Milan.

So, one week into our new venture up north, and while things were settling down on the field, my working life was about to take a turn. My boss was summoned away to another project, meaning I was put in charge. At the time it was a real shock and quite overwhelming, as it felt like I had been thrown in at the deep end. While I was given guidance on decisions I should and shouldn't make, my boss took me to one side on a rare trip to the London office and said a few words which resonated: "You're never going to please everyone all of the time." This advice proved prophetic – whenever there was disagreement or drama on the production his words were ingrained in my head. There was no time to panic – I had a production and a team to manage so it was full steam ahead.

One of the first jobs I had to organise was ensuring our entire tape library was transported up the M1 to Leeds. The set-up was very different in our new home at Yorkshire Television but after a few teething problems we made it work. In fact, in our second season in Leeds we moved to a smaller facilities house which worked better. As opposed to being based in a big news room, we had our own space and it felt more like home.

My promotion meant I had to think on my feet from day one, and I soon realised there was precious little time away from the job to spend with my now fiancée. I'd be in regular contact with James Richardson with ideas for features and jokes in the scripts and I did my best to come up with some ideas of my own. Working with him on the show gave me a real insight into his sheer professionalism and dedication to his role. He was an absolute perfectionist, which I'd seen from a distance during previous years. We didn't always agree on everything, but he was a complete genius.

Week two of the campaign saw the Marco Tardelli reign at Inter get off to a winning start, thanks to a 3–1 victory over Napoli. It was a mixed weekend for the title contenders though – champions Lazio got up and running – Hernán Crespo's first goal for the club set Sven-Göran Eriksson's side on their way to a comfortable win over Perugia.

Across the capital, big-spending Roma served notice of their intentions, earning a significant away win at Lecce with Gabriel Batistuta claiming a brace to get off the mark for his new club, the first of which was a stunning diving header.

Juventus laboured to a 2–0 win over Bari but it was a bad day for Milan as Giovanni Piacentini's last-minute winner earned a famous win for Bologna.

The following week saw Lazio suffer their first loss of the season – in Verona. Ironically, it was where the side from the capital had last tasted defeat back in March but across town Roma were on fire.

A 3–1 win over newly promoted Vicenza made it nine points out of nine for Fabio Capello's side. Gabriel Batistuta struck his third goal in as many games for Roma to put the *giallorossi* clear at the top of the table, as Juventus' 100% start ended with a 2–2 draw at Milan.

Antonio Conte's last-minute strike rescued a point for Carlo Ancelotti's side, who had to come from two goals down. The match was also notable for David Trezeguet, as the French striker scored his first goal for the *bianconeri*.

Over the opening weeks of the season though there was no stopping Roma. Despite a defeat at Inter, the *giallorossi* would win seven of their first eight matches, scoring 20 times. The run ended with a victory over Fiorentina at the Stadio Olimpico – and there were no prizes for guessing who scored the goal in a 1–0 victory.

Gabriel Batistuta's ferocious 25-yard volley won the match late on and the Argentinian showed his class by refusing to celebrate against the club where he'd made his name. The victory put Fabio Capello's side five points clear at the top.

At Juventus though things weren't so rosy and the fans' patience with coach Carlo Ancelotti was wearing thin. They were six points off the pace and also behind Udinese, who'd just beaten them in Turin, after which the Friulian club briefly led the table.

A series of uncharacteristic errors from the vastly experienced keeper Edwin van der Sar wasn't helping. The most glaring of these came in the home draw with Lazio as he let a speculative effort from Marcelo Salas go right through him. The draw at Brescia was just a sixth point in five games for the *bianconeri*.

If things were going poorly in Serie A, they were positively disastrous in the Champions League. In what was a relatively favourable-looking group (consisting of themselves, Deportivo La Coruña, Hamburg and Panathinaikos) Juventus had disaster upon disaster, humiliatingly finishing bottom of the group. The home clash with Hamburg summed up their brief challenge in Europe, featuring an horrendous performance from their Dutch keeper as well as losing both Zinedine Zidane and Edgar Davids to red cards during the first half!

The European campaign ended in suitably shambolic fashion, losing 3–1 to Panathinaikos in Athens as van der Sar and Kovačević were both sent off, making it an embarrassing five red cards in the group games for the two-time winners.

Lazio – the champions of the previous season – were faring even worse. Although they had made it through the group stage of the Champions League, their defence of the Serie A title lay in ruins by the end of November. Already nine points behind bitter rivals Roma, the very real prospect of losing the title to their hated rivals looked a distinct possibility – and with the Rome derby fast approaching things needed to change … and fast.

Down in the far south things were going far from swimmingly. Reggina – who'd surpassed all expectations by avoiding relegation in their debut Serie A season – were now in dire straits. After beating Inter on the opening day they'd go on to lose a staggering eight games in a row – and if things were going badly on the pitch they were about to get a hell of a lot worse off it.

Things came to a head in late November, when they hosted Brescia (just three points above them) at the Granillo stadium on what turned out to be one of the darkest days in the club's history. After a tight first half, Brescia broke the deadlock ten minutes into the second half through Francesco Marino. To rub salt into the wound, the forward was a local boy who'd come through the Reggina youth team.

Things quickly unravelled for the home side and after Alessandro Calori and Massimiliano Esposito had put the match beyond the home side, the supporters took matters into their own hands – throwing seats and all manner of objects onto the field. The game was briefly suspended by referee Pierluigi Collina, but with six minutes remaining and the situation escalating he had no hesitation in bringing the players off and abandoning the match. The Italian Football Federation later confirmed the 3–0 result should stand on what was a shameful day for Reggina and Italian football in general.

As we headed towards Christmas, Roma had a huge fortnight ahead of them. First up was the derby and then the last game of the calendar year would see Juventus come to town. While the *giallorossi* were the form team in Italy heading into the derby – well clear at the top of the table after winning seven of their first nine league matches – the champions went into it seven points behind their rivals and with major distractions off the field in what had been a tempestuous start to the season.

Lazio – as well as a number of other Serie A clubs – had been rocked by a passport scandal. It was alleged that several South American players (including Juan Sebastián Verón) had been issued with false European passports to get around the ruling of three non-EU players on the pitch at the same time. While Verón would eventually be cleared of all charges due to the fact that his passport was proven to be genuine, several players were hit with bans – most notably Inter's Álvaro Recoba who was to be suspended for the entire 2001/02 season.

As for the 131st Rome derby, it was as ever a tense affair in front of a packed Stadio Olimpico. In a game of few chances the critical moment came midway through the second half as Lazio defender Paolo Negro put through his own net.

Pavel Nedvěd's fierce strike, which smacked the underside of the bar, was as close as Lazio came but as the final whistle blew it was the red half of the capital celebrating wildly as they went ten points clear of the champions, whose title defence lay in tatters.

The last round of pre-Christmas fixtures saw Juventus head to the Stadio Olimpico for a huge top-of-the-table clash. Three wins in four games had seen a mini-revival for the *bianconeri* but they were still six points behind their opponents in a match they dare not lose. With so much at stake chances were few and far between. It ended goalless as Roma maintained their six-point advantage.

As the calendar year came to a close there were – as ever – plenty of other stories. Milan looked to be out of the title race after a disastrous home defeat to Perugia just before Christmas. That result left the *rossoneri* some ten points behind Roma.

Things were even worse at city rivals Inter though. They'd recorded just four wins from 12 matches and had suffered embarrassing defeats at home to Lecce as well as at rock-bottom Reggina – not to mention a 3–0 defeat at Udinese. The *nerazzurri*'s poor run of form piled the pressure on new coach Marco Tardelli.

Fiorentina were riding high in fourth place following three straight wins. They'd made history by appointing Serie A's first Turkish coach in Fatih Terim, who'd achieved great success with Galatasaray, leading them to four straight league titles. Most impressively of all he'd presided over a stunning victory the previous season for Galatasaray in the UEFA Cup as they saw off Arsenal to win a first European trophy for any Turkish side.

2001 started well too for Fiorentina as they earned a point in a thrilling 3–3 draw away to Juventus, before thrashing Milan 4–0. Enrico Chiesa started and ended the scoring in a rollercoaster of a match in Turin as Fiorentina avoided defeat at the Stadio delle Alpi for the first time.

Over at Parma the natives were getting restless. After beating Atalanta at the Ennio Tardini stadium at the start of December, they wouldn't taste victory again there until 2 February. After strugglers Vicenza and then Reggina picked up maximum points, the fans' patience snapped as they stampeded towards the changing rooms to let the coach know their thoughts in no uncertain terms.

That Reggina defeat proved a step too far for the Parma hierarchy: Alberto Malesani was sacked shortly after the final whistle. His replacement, Arrigo Sacchi, was hired to start his second spell as coach of the Emilian club. Back in 1985 he'd led the club out of the third division and very nearly to Serie A in successive seasons before

Milan came calling. After presiding over some of the most glorious times in the *rossoneri*'s history, things turned sour for Sacchi following a turbulent time coaching the national side. Despite guiding the *azzurri* to the World Cup Final in 1994, Italy's ignominious first-round exit at the European Championships in 1996 brought the curtain down on his reign with the national side and things would soon get worse.

A second spell with the *rossoneri* had proved disastrous in 1997. Under Sacchi, Milan picked up just five wins in 20 matches, the nadir being that 6–1 humiliation by Juventus at the San Siro in what was the club's heaviest ever Serie A defeat.

Now he was back with Parma too for a second time, but with the club entrenched in mid-table, European qualification looked to be the best they could hope for. His reign at the Ennio Tardini stadium would be a fleeting one though, and just 23 days after his appointment he resigned for personal reasons, following defeat by Udinese in the Coppa Italia semi-finals.

At the top Roma were having a slight wobble. They kicked off the calendar year with victory at Atalanta but that was followed by a disappointing home draw with rock-bottom Bari and then defeat at Milan on the same day Juventus exorcised a few demons by winning in Perugia in front of the *Football Italia* cameras – Filippo Inzaghi scoring the only goal.

That victory for the *bianconeri* saw the gap at the top cut to three points but it wouldn't last long as the following week it was back up to six following Roma's victory in Parma and Juventus' defeat at Atalanta. The *bianconeri* actually went ahead with just 17 minutes left in Bergamo only for goals from Stefano Lorenzi and Nicola Ventola to turn the match on its head.

It meant Roma were winter champions but Fabio Capello and his men knew there was a long way to go if they were to secure a first scudetto since 1983, and they started the second half of the campaign like an express train – winning five successive matches including a dramatic five-goal thriller with Inter at the Stadio Olimpico.

Across town it was an end of an era as Lazio parted company with title-winning coach Sven-Göran Eriksson. The home defeat by Napoli left the champions nine points adrift of the leaders and coming so soon after their derby defeat the club hierarchy felt it was the moment to call time on the coach's reign.

After a period of unparalleled success in the club's history which had brought seven trophies (a scudetto, two Coppa Italia titles, the Cup Winners' Cup, UEFA Super Cup as well as two Italian Super Cups) it was time to say farewell. Whether it was Lazio's indifferent form or the fact that Roma were seemingly on their way to take Lazio's scudetto crown – or maybe both – we'll never know, but at the time it certainly felt as if Roma's incredible resurgence had plenty to do with it. The new man in the Lazio dugout was Dino Zoff, back for an astonishing third stint as boss, until the end of the season. He would preside over a dramatic return to form for the champions, who won seven of the next eight matches under the veteran coach.

Across the capital Roma were going from strength to strength to maintain a firm grip on the Serie A leadership. Juventus, however, were just about managing to match their remarkable sequence of results so by mid-March the gap was still six points. Things would change dramatically in week 23. In the afternoon Roma dropped their first points in six weeks following a goalless draw at Reggina, meaning Juventus could cut the gap to four if they could win in the evening at Roma's bitter rivals Lazio.

It left *giallorossi* fans in the unique situation of having to support their hated rivals. It turned into a pivotal night in the title race as Juventus were ripped apart by the champions with Pavel Nedvěd and Hernán Crespo scoring twice each in a 4–1 rout. Alessandro Del Piero's stunning strike proved a mere consolation on a hugely damaging night for Juve's title hopes.

A fortnight later and Roma moved further clear. A half-time one-goal deficit at home to Verona was turned into a comfortable 3–1 win on the same day Juventus hosted Brescia in Turin. For a long time, it looked like Gianluca Zambrotta's first-half goal would be enough, but with just five minutes remaining substitute Roberto Baggio turned the clock back to score a stunning late equaliser for Brescia. After being in charge of the Perugia side that had left Juventus shattered on the final day of the previous season, it was Carlo Mazzone again –

now coaching Brescia – who would strike another dagger into the heart of the *bianconeri*'s title dreams. It all meant the *giallorossi* were nine now points clear, their biggest lead of the season.

The previous campaign had seen Juventus boast a similar advantage at almost exactly the same stage themselves, and the following week would see the *bianconeri* close the gap. Their next match took them to the Marcantonio Bentegodi stadium – where Verona had shocked them almost a year earlier with a defeat that ultimately cost them the title.

This time though Verona were in a desperate battle to avoid the drop and Alessandro Del Piero's penalty on the stroke of half time proved to be the only goal. Just 24 hours later Roma travelled to Fiorentina, who'd recently sacked their coach Fatih Terim following a string of disagreements with the club's hierarchy.

The new man in the hotseat was Roberto Mancini in what was the first coaching role of his own, having been Sven-Göran Eriksson's assistant at Lazio. His former employers would have been delighted with his side's performance against the league leaders, as Roma went down to only a third Serie A defeat of the season, as Gabriel Batistuta endured a miserable return to the city where he'd made his name.

Juventus were pretty pleased with that result too and the gap would go down to just four points the following weekend as an injury-time own goal rescued Roma from back-to-back defeats against Perugia. On the same day Juventus comfortably saw off Inter, but the lead would only stay at four points for a week following Juve's goalless draw at Parma.

There were now just seven matches remaining and the following fortnight was – in many people's minds – where the title was going to be won and lost.

First up Juventus hosted struggling Lecce before Roma faced Lazio in a huge Rome derby. Seven days later Roma would be heading to Turin for a match of epic proportions. With so much at stake and with tensions running high, there were more than a few twists and turns in the title race.

First up was Juventus versus Lecce in Turin. It looked – on paper – a home banker. Lecce hadn't won on their travels for five and a half months, during which time Juventus were unbeaten at the Stadio delle Alpi. Added to that Juventus had trounced Lecce at the Via del Mare stadium in mid-December and they had never beaten the *bianconeri* away from home.

When Igor Tudor fired the *bianconeri* ahead after 40 minutes it seemed the home side were on course for another routine victory. Astonishingly though, Lecce were level just 15 seconds after the restart through Alessandro Conticchio's spectacular diving header.

The real drama came late on, as Filippo Inzaghi fired a penalty against the frame of the goal and would then fire a shot against the very same post with the last kick of the game in what was – truth be told – a disastrous afternoon for Juventus. The events of the evening would render those misses even more crucial.

Roma went into the derby looking for a first league double over their city rivals in over 40 years. The *giallorossi* knew that a win would take them eight points clear of Juventus ahead of their massive showdown in Turin seven days later.

A tense, scoreless first half gave no hint of what was to come as within ten minutes of the restart Roma were two goals up and looking set to go eight points clear. It stayed that way until 12 minutes from time, which was when Lazio's Czech midfielder Pavel Nedvěd halved the deficit, setting up a tense final few minutes.

Rome clung on to their lead until the last 30 seconds of added time. Substitute Lucas Castromán's ferocious strike from the edge of the box secured a dramatic point for Lazio. Roma were shattered as their lead over Juventus remained six points.

Seven days later all roads led to Turin for what was surely the final opportunity for Juventus to catch up with Roma in the title race. Both sides had a relatively straightforward run-in and with five games remaining after this crucial meeting Carlo Ancelotti's side knew a win would not only put some real pressure on the league leaders but give them some serious momentum over the final weeks of the campaign.

In front of a sold-out Stadio delle Alpi, Juventus could not have wished for a better start. With just four minutes on the clock Zinedine Zidane crossed in for Alessandro Del Piero to head home and from the restart the home side would incredibly go two up. Roma keeper Francesco Antonioli was completely wrong-footed by Zidane's shot from the edge of the box to send the home fans into delirium.

The league leaders just couldn't get a foothold in the game and as the sides went in at half time Roma boss Fabio Capello knew he had to do something if his side were to get back into it. He hauled off striker Marco Delvecchio and introduced leading scorer Vincenzo Montella to the fray.

It had little impact though. Juventus were happy to sit back and protect their lead as Roma showed precious little up front to worry Edwin van der Sar in the Juventus goal. On came Hidetoshi Nakata – and with 11 minutes remaining the Japanese midfielder scored a stunning goal – beating Juve's keeper from all of 25 yards – to set up a thrilling conclusion.

Roma desperately poured forward in search of the equaliser and it came dramatically in stoppage time. Nakata tried his luck again from long range. Van der Sar could only parry it into the path of Montella, who scored his most important goal of the season to rescue a point for Roma, who somehow maintained their six-point lead. The game looked up for Juventus.

Sneaking up under the radar though were Lazio. Dino Zoff had somehow turned their season around after the sacking of Sven-Göran Eriksson and their win over Bari on the same day had actually seen them overhaul Juventus to go five points behind Roma.

With three games to go things remained unchanged – Roma five points clear – until Milan came to the Stadio Olimpico. The *rossoneri* had been revitalised since Cesare Maldini (father of their legendary left back Paolo) had replaced Alberto Zaccheroni. Their recent emphatic six-goal thrashing of city rivals Inter was testament to the club's revival.

So, they were dangerous opponents for Roma, and shortly before the interval Francesco Coco headed in from a corner to put the visitors ahead.

Milan's one-goal lead remained intact until midway through the second half, when Vincenzo Montella scored one of the goals of the season. The striker's inch-perfect chip saw the *giallorossi* draw level and even though the visitors hit the post late on the match ended all square.

On the same evening Juventus took full advantage of Roma's slip up. David Trezeguet's goal was enough to see off Perugia in Turin. The *bianconeri* moved to within four points of Roma as Lazio were denied a win over Inter, thanks to Stéphane Dalmat's stunning strike in added time.

That match had been played in Bari following an horrific incident at the start of May during Inter's win over Atalanta at the San Siro. A vespa was thrown from the upper tier of the San Siro onto the terrified fans below. Quite how it was smuggled into the stadium was another matter entirely as the Italian Football Federation punished Inter by making them play their next two home games on neutral ground. It was a pretty shameful day for Italian football with hooliganism once more rearing its ugly head.

In the title race, there were just two games remaining and Roma's penultimate clash took them to Napoli who were in a desperate battle to avoid relegation in what was their first season back in the top flight. Roma knew that a defeat for Juventus in Vicenza would see them crowed champions regardless of the outcome in Naples.

It wouldn't turn out that way though. Juventus cruised to a 3–0 win – scoring their goals in a 15-minute spell either side of half time – and things were far tougher for the *giallorossi* 700 kilometres south.

Nicola Amoruso's strike was cancelled out by Gabriel Batistuta before half time. Francesco Totti put the league leaders in front but Napoli would ultimately salvage a draw. Fabio Pecchia's late free kick somehow squeezed under Francesco Antonioli to halve the gap to two points with just a game to play. Vincenzo Montella's late goal in Turin was worth its weight in gold now as Roma knew a win over Parma would see them end their 18-year wait for the scudetto.

So, to 17 June, and the final day of a long season. Roma knew a win over Parma at the Stadio Olimpico would be enough for the title. With their visitors having nothing to play for after securing their place in the Champions League qualifying rounds, the result seemed a formality. In the back of their minds though the *giallorossi* knew that Juventus would almost certainly pick up three points of their own at home to Atalanta who – just like Parma – had nothing riding on the game.

With their adoring fans roaring them on, the league leaders put in a near-perfect performance. First-half goals from Francesco Totti and Vincenzo Montella all but secured the title before the break. When Gabriel Batistuta struck the third goal 13 minutes from time the party could really get started. Marco Di Vaio's late consolation goal mattered little.

Up in Turin there were more tears for the *bianconeri* who'd been left shattered on the final day by a Roman side for the second successive year. This time though nobody could question that Roma thoroughly deserved the scudetto. Having been at the top of the table pretty much the whole way through, it was an outstanding triumph for Fabio Capello and his men. The coach with the Midas touch was now able to boast a fifth scudetto as he brought the title back to Roma for the first time in almost two decades.

The celebrations went on for weeks. Actress Sabrina Ferilli – a lifelong Roma fan and film star – carried out her pledge to go topless at the Circus Maximus if her side won the scudetto, in front of the club's raucous fans.

Whatever the players achieved in the rest of their playing careers, they would forever be heroes in the eyes of the *giallorossi*'s passionate supporters. Despite their big spending the previous summer, nobody had predicted this title for Roma.

As for Juventus, the inquest went on as they endured a third consecutive trophyless season. Unsurprisingly it was Carlo Ancelotti who paid the price – another second-place finish wasn't enough to save his job, despite recently signing a two-year extension to his contract. In a rather undignified manner his departure was made public at half-time during the win over Atalanta on the final day of the season.

Rome was not only the capital of the country but it was now the home of *calcio* too, with its teams capturing consecutive scudetti. The big question was: what could the northern powerhouses do about it?

9

LA PARTITA È FINITA

The 2000/01 season eventually wound down in late June as Verona prevailed in a tension-riddled two-legged play-off with Reggina. With Bari and Napoli also relegated it left only Lecce representing the south of Italy in Serie A.

It all meant a short summer break for Italian sides with the 2001/02 season having to start in late August in order that it could be finished in time for the upcoming World Cup in Japan and South Korea.

Despite the off season being so short there were a huge number of personnel changes right across Serie A – and none were bigger at the northern trio of Juventus, Inter and Milan, who were each desperate to end the recent transfer of power to the capital.

Nowhere were the changes bigger than at Juventus. Three consecutive barren seasons had meant the end for Carlo Ancelotti. His association with Milan meant he was never really accepted by a large percentage of *bianconeri* fans. As President Umberto Agnelli said: "The reason for Ancelotti's departure is that it is difficult to work in a city where the great part of the fans and press are against you."

Two and a half years after resigning from Juventus – and following an unsuccessful spell as Inter coach – Marcello Lippi returned to the scene of his greatest triumphs, but it wasn't just in the dugout where there'd be a new man. On the field, there were all manner of changes as the club put together a squad that they hoped would return them to the top of the Italian game. They'd have to do it, however, without the mercurial Zinedine Zidane. He was off to Real Madrid for a world record fee of £46 million as the World Cup and European Championship winner left after five seasons in Turin.

His replacement was Pavel Nedvěd who joined after a hugely successful time with Lazio, where he'd won titles both at home and abroad. The fee was £25 million and he'd be joined at Juventus by former Lazio team mate – Chilean striker Marcelo Salas. He signed for £8 million, with striker Darko Kovačević heading in the opposite direction.

But Juventus hadn't yet finished splashing the cash yet, and were about to sign some of the top talent from Parma too. In came keeper Gianluigi Buffon for over £30 million and he'd be joined by French defender Lilian Thuram for £23 million.

Over at Milan changes were afoot too. After Cesare Maldini's brief role as caretaker there was a new man in the hotseat at the San Siro – Fatih Terim. Despite falling out with the Fiorentina hierarchy the previous season, the *rossoneri* saw him as the man to get them challenging for the title once again. Also making the move from Tuscany was midfield playmaker Rui Costa, after seven largely successful seasons in Florence.

The biggest signing of all though was still to come as Milan managed to lure Filippo Inzaghi away from Juventus. The fee was around £17 million and after being largely relegated to the bench following the arrival of David Trezeguet the previous summer – not to mention his now-fractious relationship with Alessandro Del Piero – the move made sense for all parties.

Inzaghi would be joined at the *rossoneri* by Andrea Pirlo. He'd swapped from the blue to the red half of the San Siro and it'd be the start of a career that would see him become a Milan legend.

Over at Inter there was also a new coach as Marco Tardelli was replaced by Héctor Cúper. The Argentinian had made his name in the Champions League – defying the odds by taking Valencia to consecutive finals during his two-year reign at the Mestalla.

After being well beaten by Real Madrid (in what was a first ever all-Spanish final in the competition in 2000) they met Bayern Munich the following year in a final played (ironically as it turned out) at the San Siro. Once again though it ended in heartbreak for the Spanish side, as they were beaten in a dramatic penalty shoot-out.

That would be his final act with Valencia and his first act as coach of Inter would be to strengthen the attack. The club had struggled for goals in the previous campaign but could now boast a wealth of talent, starting with their talisman.

Ronaldo would soon be back from his horrific knee injury and he would spearhead an attack also boasting the likes of Christian Vieri, Nicola Ventola and Mohamed Kallon. They'd also have Álvaro Recoba back – his one-year ban for the false passport scandal having been reduced to just four months on appeal.

There were few changes at champions Roma, but Fabio Capello had bolstered his attacking options – snapping up Antonio Cassano from Bari, considered one of the brightest young talents in Italy.

Somewhat surprisingly Capello let Hidetoshi Nakata leave for Parma. The Japanese midfielder had, over the closing weeks of the previous season, played a pivotal role in Roma securing the scudetto, most notably scoring and assisting Vincenzo Montella's equaliser in the crucial match away to Juventus. As for Parma, minus Buffon and Thuram – two of their biggest names – it'd prove to be a turbulent season at the Ennio Tardini stadium. Three coaches came and went in what would be Parma's lowest league placing since their arrival in Serie A back in 1990.

There was no doubt about the fairytale story though, as we had a team about to embark on their maiden season in Italy's top flight. They came from a very small corner of the city of Verona, home to just 4,500 people. The club was called Chievo and they were about to make quite a splash in Italy's top flight. They only became professional in the mid-1980s and after reaching the giddy heights of Serie B in 1994 they'd spend seven years in Italy's second division.

In 2001 – after his first season as coach – Luigi Delneri achieved the miracle, as Chievo achieved promotion to Serie A in what was a hugely competitive Serie B, which featured ten sides that had competed in Italy's top flight over the previous decade. More familiar names such as Genoa, Sampdoria and Cagliari all missed out.

The President of the new boys – Luca Campedelli – was a local man who had followed in his father Luigi's footsteps to become Serie A's youngest ever President, aged just 23. Luigi Campedelli had passed away in 1992 following a heart attack, leaving Luca not only in charge of the football club but also the hugely successful company – Paluani. The organisation specialises in Italian cakes, most notably the panettone, millions of which are sold globally around Christmas time.

The new President's philosophy – as his father had hoped – was to never put the family business at risk by paying lavish fees on players and wages for the club. With Chievo unlikely to attract big crowds at the 40,000-capacity Marcantonio Bentegodi stadium (except for when the likes of Juventus plus the Milan and Rome clubs were in town) it was a prudent and sensible approach.

Italian football was sadly now gaining a reputation for racism and fan violence but this new club were a breath of fresh air, priding themselves on a friendly, warm atmosphere, making themselves regularly accessible for the media. On several occasions, the *Gazzetta* crew would be heading up to Verona for shoots. Whether we'd be interviewing players, coach Delneri or indeed the owner, they always made time for us. They were loving the exposure of being in the company of the country's big guns. If you weren't from Verona, they wanted Chievo to be your second team.

Across town at city rivals Verona there were dramatic changes afoot. Their coach Alberto Malesani – Verona born and bred – had actually started cutting his coaching teeth with Chievo, guiding the club into Serie B in his first season with them back in 1993. Now though, he was with the more established Veronese side. In the city – most famous for being the setting of *Romeo and Juliet* – there was a veritable revolution taking place, and just like in the Shakespeare classic the emphasis was on youth, particularly up front – boasting the likes of Argentinian winger Mauro Camoranesi – who'd go on to become a scudetto winner with Juventus – and up front Romanian international Adrian Mutu and Alberto Gilardino, who would win the Champions League with Milan and also the 2006 World Cup with the Italian national side.

The 2001/02 season was the final year of Channel 4's *Football Italia* contract, and as it turned out it wasn't renewed and so it sadly proved to be the conclusion of our coverage of Italian football. There had been signs that this was on the cards several times over the previous 12 months or so. There wasn't much interest from the channel in showing any of the night matches, which had been broadcast in previous years. The coverage was better, the crowds were bigger, the atmosphere was louder but there was a general impression – which the staff felt – that the production was now on borrowed time.

Several times over the previous couple of years there was no live game at the weekend and there'd been a growing tendency for the match of the week to be shown as late-night highlights. The huge title-deciding clashes between Juventus and Lazio in 2000, as well as Juventus against Roma a year later, weren't shown live, just as midnight highlights shows.

Therefore, it didn't really come as much of a surprise when we discovered in the summer of 2001 that there wouldn't be any more live games, and so *Football Italia – La Partita* was created. This would involve extended highlights of the best afternoon match as well as the night match and would finish with the goals round-up from the remaining seven games. James Richardson would record some links in a similar way to his "news of the week" on *Gazzetta*, sat outside a Roman café with either an ice cream or a pizza for company. Sometimes there'd be a post-work carafe of chianti lurking too!

The good news was that *Gazzetta* was still thriving – its loyal audience lapping up their weekly fix of Italian football, newspapers and all our regular features, not to mention plenty of witticism from James along the way. Admittedly it faced some tough competition on the airwaves on a Saturday morning, but it wasn't just our regular audience who watched the programme religiously. For a football fan, it was an institution on matchday back here in the United Kingdom, and we had a new voice too as broadcaster Jonny Gould would come to Leeds on the Friday edit day. He was hugely experienced and had a namesake who presented baseball on another channel, but his passion for the game made him the perfect choice. Just after he started I discovered he'd been a huge fan of the show since its inception a decade earlier.

While the production remained in Leeds for *Gazzetta*, it was decided that *La Partita* would be produced in London. That proved to be a popular decision for the talent in particular, most of whom had grown increasingly tired of the weekly trips up the M1.

So, to the big kick-off. Week one focused on the reigning champions – Roma. They travelled north to take on Verona in the big night match while we also featured Marcello Lippi's second debut with Juventus, as they hosted newly promoted Venezia, and it would be the *bianconeri* who'd be the biggest winners on the opening weekend. David Trezeguet and Alessandro Del Piero picking up a couple of goals apiece in a 4–0 rout.

Inter also scored four in their thrashing of Perugia, while Roma kicked off their title defence with a disappointing 1–1 draw away to Verona. The biggest story of the day though belonged to their cross-city rivals – Chievo – whose debut match in Italy's top flight saw them ease to a 2–0 win at Fiorentina. Goals from Simone Perrotta and Massimo Marazzina provided the upset of the opening weekend – and if anyone thought that result was a one-off they'd be in for a shock.

Week two would see just two clubs maintain a 100% start. Juventus won at Atalanta and they were joined at the top of the table by new boys Chievo who were in dreamland after a 2–0 win over Bologna. As fate would have it, the following weekend would see them meet in Turin in what was the biggest night in Chievo's short history.

With both sides yet to concede, one might have expected a cagey affair – it was anything but. The evening got off to a sombre start with teams, staff and supporters paying their respects to the 3,000 people who had horrifically lost their lives in the 9/11 attacks.

The new boys took the game to Juventus from the off, and would incredibly find themselves two goals in front after just 20 minutes, both coming from Massimo Marazzina. His first followed an uncharacteristic error from Gianluigi Buffon and when he swept home the second, Luigi Delneri's side were in dreamland.

Two minutes later though Alessio Tacchinardi's volley brought a sense of order to proceedings and by the interval the 25-time champions would be level through centre half Igor Tudor. A late penalty from Marcelo Salas completed the turnaround as Marcello Lippi's side made it three wins out of three.

While things were going to plan up in Turin, they were far from it in the capital, the home of the two most recent champions. It was the scudetto holders Roma who were really struggling though, the loss at newly promoted Piacenza making it just two points from the first three games.

As for Lazio, being held to a goalless draw by Torino and then humiliatingly losing 3–1 at home to Nantes in the Champions League, meant the end for coach Dino Zoff. He was replaced by former Udinese and Milan coach Alberto Zaccheroni, who, to start with couldn't turn around Lazio's league form either. A 2–0 win over Atalanta saw him get a victory at the fourth attempt.

That poor start was nothing compared to promoted Venezia though. Their return to Serie A would be a brief one as they were relegated by quite some distance. Their early-season form set the tone for an horrific campaign, losing their first six matches and incredibly not recording a victory until just before Christmas. It'd be the first of just three in the entire season.

Inter were the team setting the pace, winning five of their first six matches. The last of those – against Verona – saw Héctor Cúper's side cruise to a 3–0 win, in a match which saw the hugely anticipated return of their talisman. Ronaldo struck twice in the second half with two classic finishes to seal what was a routine win for the *nerazzurri*.

While Inter were flying, Juventus' momentum suddenly stalled. A goalless draw at Lecce (during which they had both Paolo Montero and Edgar Davids sent off) was followed by a 2–0 home defeat to champions Roma. So the *bianconeri* would head into the first *Derby della Mole* of the season not in the best of form. As for Torino, they'd just beaten Parma to record their first win of the season.

What followed was one of the most dramatic Turin derbies in history and the archetypal game of two halves. Juventus roared into a three-goal lead after just 25 minutes. Two from Alessandro Del Piero and another for Igor Tudor had the *bianconeri* all but out of sight. It remained that way until the interval, and in the second half Torino looked a completely different side. Christian Lucarelli's strike just before the hour gave the *granata* hope. A Marco Ferrante penalty made it 3–2 with 20 minutes left and astonishingly Torino were level seven minutes from time through Riccardo Maspero.

Remarkably the drama was still not over. With just three minutes remaining Igor Tudor's shirt was tugged and Juventus had the chance to win the game from the penalty spot amid huge protests from their opponents. However, Marcelo Salas sent his effort soaring over the crossbar, leaving Torino to celebrate an unexpected point.

That draw came in the middle of a complete loss of form for the *bianconeri*. After opening the season with three straight wins, they would only pick up six points from the next seven games, before finally recording a victory in mid-November at home to Parma. It was a first league win for Marcello Lippi's side in two months.

Up in Milan, two foreign coaches were leading their sides into a first *Derby della Madonnina.* This particular derby is named after statue of the Virgin Mary, which sits at the top of the city's famous Duomo. Both sides would go into this latest meeting in contrasting form. Héctor Cúper's Inter were a point clear of surprise package Chievo at the top of the Serie A table and unbeaten, whereas their city rivals – now under the leadership of Fatih Terim – were five points back and winless in their last three games, the last of which had seen them embarrassingly become the first side to drop points against rock-bottom Venezia.

As is often said though, in a derby form goes out of the window, and this meeting of two of Italian football's giants would be testament to that. The first half however, went to script. Nicola Ventola's tap-in early on saw the league leaders off to a flier but after half time the match would be turned on its head. Three goals in seven minutes – from Andriy Shevchenko, half-time substitute Cosmin Contra and Filippo Inzaghi – put Milan in control. A fourth from Shevchenko sealed it and despite Mohamed Kallon's late consolation Inter were consigned to a first league defeat on what was a triumphant night for Fatih Terim and his side.

The derby focus switched to the capital the following week as the previous two champions clashed, and it was Roma who prevailed thanks to second-half goals from Marco Delvecchio and Francesco Totti.

Even though both sides from Genoa remained in Serie B, the 2001/02 campaign saw a huge number of derbies in Serie A, and while the traditional cross-city clashes in Milan, Turin and Rome took centre stage, not all of them were as high-profile but they often had no end of drama.

Brescia and Atalanta (from Bergamo) are separated by the best part of 50 kilometres and while they don't hail from the same city, when they meet it's usually fiery both on and off the field. The rivalry between the two towns goes back almost 900 years, as in 1126 some land in Brescia went up for sale and Bergamo bought it to give themselves a territorial advantage that only ceased 30 years later when the Romanian emperor Frederick I returned the land to Brescia. Not long after that, war broke out between the two and Brescia invaded the province of Bergamo, inflicting a resounding defeat on the *Bergamaschi*, resulting in the deaths of 2,500 people. Peace was eventually brought to the region but it didn't last long and in 1237 came the infamous Battle of Cortenuova, where the *Bergamaschi* finally defeated the Guelfs of Brescia.

To this day the bitterness between the two cities is as strong as ever. Atalanta fans call their rivals "pigs" due to the fact that Brescia has more pigs than people, while Brescia's riposte to that is to call their rivals "rabbits". This all stems back to the 1930s when during a derby at Brescia's Rigamonti stadium the home fans released hundreds of rabbits onto the pitch during the match. Several months later Atalanta subsequently released dozens of pigs into the away stand at the return fixture!

The 2000/01 season had seen Atalanta complete a league double over their bitter rivals in what was Brescia's first season back in Italy's top flight following a two-year absence. So the Bresciani were hell-bent on revenge heading into their first meeting of the 2001/02 season at their Rigamonti stadium, a match which is still talked about for one particular incident.

Things started well for the home side with Roberto Baggio volleying home at the far post to put his side into the lead. However, their joy would be short lived as goals from Luigi Sala, Cristiano Doni and Gianni Comandini had the visitors in complete control at the break – the Bergamaschi looking strong favourites to seal a third straight win over their rivals. Following some stirring words from coach Carlo Mazzone, the home side came out revitalised after the interval as the temperature heated up both on and off the field. Insult after insult rained down on the Brescia boss (some shamefully involving his mother) from the visiting supporters. When Roberto Baggio's second of the game made it 3–2 with a quarter of an hour remaining, Mazzone shouted to the Atalanta fans that he'd be coming over when – not if – the home side equalised.

Indeed, that leveller arrived deep into stoppage time as Roberto Baggio's free kick evaded everyone to complete his hat-trick and send Mazzone berserk. Despite their attempts to hold back the veteran coach, Mazzone was on a one-man mission to let the Atalanta fans know exactly what he thought of them – angrily shaking his fist while the *Bergamaschi* threw anything they could at him.

Upon returning to the dugout, referee Pierluigi Collina had little option but to show Mazzone the red card, which the coach took in good grace.

Eleven weeks into the new season we'd had derbies in Turin, Milan, Rome (where Roma had inflicted yet more pain on Lazio) as well as the heated Brescia versus Atalanta affair. One remained in the first half of the season and it took place at the Marcantonio Bentegodi stadium in mid-November. It'd be an historic one as Verona clashed with Chievo for the first time in Serie A.

Chievo's dream start to life in the top flight had yielded seven wins from their opening ten matches to leave the Serie A new boys two points clear of Inter and astonishingly leading the title race. Verona, meanwhile, lay ten points behind their city rivals, who were revelling in their glorious start as they headed into a first ever *Derby della Scala* in Serie A.

"Donkeys will fly before Chievo are in Serie A" claimed the Verona fans in years gone by, so the Serie A new boys decided to poke fun at their rivals by giving themselves the nickname the "flying donkeys". Not only that, but in this first top-flight derby Chievo took the opportunity to remind their more established neighbours of that statement, suspending miniature flying donkeys from the roof of the Marcantonio Bentegodi stadium prior to kick off.

Once the action started the match more than justified all the hype. Chievo struck twice in four minutes – from Brazilian winger Eriberto and then captain Eugenio Corini from the penalty spot, his goal being all the sweeter as he'd joined Chievo from Verona some three years earlier.

Verona weren't lying down though – this was the biggest derby the city had ever seen, and the momentum changed just before the break. Adrian Mutu was upended by Paolo Foglio and Massimo Oddo halved the deficit from the spot. The flying donkeys were really up against it when star striker Massimo Marazzina saw red for a crude challenge on Mauro Camoranesi.

Verona took full advantage, levelling with 19 minutes left in bizarre circumstances. Left back Salvatore Lanna took a wild swipe at the ball and swiftly collapsed to the deck as the ball completely wrong-footed keeper Cristiano Lupatelli to make it two apiece in the unlikeliest of circumstances. There was only going to be one winner now and within two minutes Verona had turned the match completely on its head with Mauro Camoranesi stabbing home what would prove to be the winner.

Chievo didn't let this setback derail them though – bouncing back the following week at home to Perugia. While things were going beyond all expectations for them, it wasn't the same for everyone else and for one of the title favourites in particular.

Despite their thrilling derby win it had been a less than impressive start to the season for Milan. As well as a humiliating defeat at Perugia there had been dropped points at home – against Bologna and worse still at home to a Venezia side who'd lost their first six games before their trip to the San Siro. These results had put new boss Fatih Terim under pressure just a few months into his reign and heading to Torino a result was needed more than ever.

However, another damaging defeat would prove to be the end for the Turk. Cristiano Lucarelli's strike gave Torino a first-half advantage and Terim's fate was sealed after Filippo Inzaghi blazed a late penalty over the bar. Terim's sacking came as a result of what was deemed overly attack-minded tactics, and his cause wasn't helped by his insistence of playing this brand of football ahead of results.

His replacement was legendary *rossoneri* midfielder Carlo Ancelotti. Five months after his sacking at Juventus he was about to start what would prove to be a glittering eight-year spell as Milan coach. It was a period where he'd lose the "nearly man" tag he'd acquired at Parma and Juventus – winning major trophies at home and abroad – and while his reign with the *rossoneri* would get off to a less-than-convincing start (a goalless draw at home to Piacenza) things would soon pick up for the 16-time champions.

The same could not be said in Florence. A disappointing start to the season would escalate into a full-blown crisis both on and off the field. A 3–1 win over Venezia in late September looked to be a step in the right direction but the ramifications of an horrendous injury to star striker Enrico Chiesa would prove disastrous for the *viola*. Shortly after firing them into an early lead, he damaged tendons in his knee – an injury that would rule him out for the rest of the season.

By the time we got to the New Year, Fiorentina's season was starting to unravel, and they would go on to record just one win in the final 19 matches as they nosedived to relegation. After scoring nine times in the opening five rounds with Chiesa they would only muster another 20 in the remaining 29 matches. Quite simply the striker's goals were irreplaceable.

While things were going disastrously on the field, Fiorentina's cause was in turmoil off it. Following a police raid on club President Vittorio Cecchi Gori's house in 2001, it transpired that Fiorentina's finances were in a dire state – in debt to the tune of £40 million. Cecchi Gori was alleged to have channelled money from the club to fund his film production business.

All of this would result in the club suffering a disastrous season, and following relegation in May 2002 they didn't even have the funds to start the new campaign in Serie B. The club was declared bankrupt and was liquidated that summer. As a result, a new club was formed and Florentina Viola was forced to fight its way back from Serie C2 –

Italy's fourth division. They'd eventually be renamed ACF Fiorentina and within a few years would be back among the top Italian sides in Serie A.

Back on the field there was still British interest in Serie A with Udinese being coached by the vastly experienced Roy Hodgson – back for a third stint in Italy. While he'd achieved some decent results for his new club, things were about to turn sour. A solid start to the season saw the club comfortably placed in mid-table, but following a dramatic late victory over Verona in early December the talk wasn't of on-field events. A remark in which he stated he regretted joining the club in the summer and called Udinese "a strange club" obviously didn't go down well with players, officials or supporters. Club owner Giampaolo Pozzo was said to be furious and the former Inter boss was immediately replaced by Giampiero Ventura.

That defeat at Udinese was symptomatic of Verona's season as late goals conceded proved to be their Achilles heel. It had already cost them victory against both Parma and Juventus but the real horror show came at Torino at the end of November. Adrian Mutu's early strike had put Verona into the lead – an advantage they held for an hour – before the roof fell in on them. After Marco Ferrante had levelled for the hosts, the visitors incredibly conceded four goals in the final 15 minutes to eventually go down to a 5–1 drubbing.

As the Serie A season headed towards the Christmas break it was getting ever tighter at the top. Inter were still leading the way and after their stunning defeat in the Milan derby had hit a rich vein of form. Just a week before their final game of 2001 they hosted the team that had without question been the story of the season – Chievo.

A fortnight earlier the flying donkeys had gone down to Milan in a five-goal thriller but were now back at the San Siro to face the sternest test of their maiden Serie A season. The new boys would go on to record one of the biggest upsets of the season – Massimo Marazzina's strike early in the second half earning the visitors a stunning 2–1 victory as they briefly returned to the Serie A summit.

However, the following week would see Chievo going down 3–0 at home to Roma and after Inter scraped a 3–2 win at Piacenza it'd be

Inter leading the way going into the New Year with just two points separating themselves, Chievo and Roma at the top.

What of Juventus though? After a disappointing run of form in the autumn the *bianconeri* would register seven successive wins either side of Christmas to move to within a point of the top. Their star striker David Trezeguet would score six times in that run – which included an impressive win at Chievo as the fight for the title really started to hot up.

After their heroics in the opening half of the season it was unsurprising that the New Year would see Chievo fall away in the race for the title. After beating Atalanta in their first match of 2002 they wouldn't win again for well over two months. Their results though were completely overshadowed by the tragic events of 2 March – a day which sent the world of Italian football into mourning as their flying winger – Jason Mayélé tragically lost his life in a car accident. The club made the decision to retire his number 30 shirt as a mark of respect.

With Chievo predictably unable to repeat their incredible first half of the season it would still see them qualify for European football in a first ever Serie A campaign. Not only that, there'd be tears on the other side of the city as Verona would be relegated. The differences between the two clubs' fortunes couldn't have been more stark. Finally, Chievo were the top dogs in Verona and they were relishing it.

At the very top, the 2001/02 season was to become a thrilling three-horse race between Inter, defending champions Roma and Juventus. The *nerazzurri* started the New Year after edging out Piacenza in a five-goal thriller but that winning feeling wouldn't last. A draw at rock-bottom Venezia would be followed by a stalemate at home to Torino and then defeat in Bologna.

Over the same period Juventus would be stringing together six consecutive wins and Roma were in impressive form too, so at the start of February, Roma held a one-point advantage over their northern rivals ahead of a critical period of the season. All three would be involved in huge local derbies over three weekends as the title race really started to hot up.

This trilogy of derbies started in Turin, where Juventus had a score to settle after blowing a three-goal lead against their city rivals earlier in the season, and once again it would be a dramatic and hugely controversial encounter. David Trezeguet's early strike got the *bianconeri* off to the perfect start but the match would be turned on its head after the break. An uncharacteristic error from Lilian Thuram set up Marco Ferrante for the equaliser and when Benoît Cauet stunningly fired the *granata* ahead with just ten minutes remaining Torino were on course for a first *Derby della Mole* victory in seven years. The match, however, would end among unsavoury scenes, following Enzo Maresca's stunning header. The former West Bromwich Albion midfielder mocked the "bull horn" celebration of Torino forward Marco Ferrante. The bull is one of the symbols of the *granata* – hence the "Toro" nickname and provoked heated scenes at the full-time whistle. In later years Maresca nearly signed for Torino but this episode hadn't been forgiven or forgotten by the club's supporters and the deal broke down.

Despite Maresca's late heroics it was another two points dropped for Marcello Lippi's side, although they remained just a point behind joint leaders Inter and Roma. The following weekend saw Inter gain revenge for their derby defeat back in October, beating Milan 1–0 thanks to a late goal from Christian Vieri. The gap remained one point though – Juventus scraped home against Bologna after a dramatic own goal by Massimo Tarantino late on. The defender – standing in oceans of space in the penalty area – astonishingly headed past bewildered former Inter keeper Gianluca Pagliuca with just a couple of minutes remaining to earn Juventus a priceless victory, as the *bianconeri* stayed just a point back from Inter ahead of a mouthwatering *Derby d'Italia* at the San Siro seven days later.

As well as it being a huge – potentially decisive – game in the fight for the scudetto, it would also be the first time Marcello Lippi had returned to face Inter at the San Siro since his controversial departure almost 18 months earlier. The match didn't disappoint.

Inter got off to a dream start. Clarence Seedorf's explosive volley put the *nerazzurri* ahead after just six minutes, but the lead wouldn't last long. David Trezeguet would equalise within the first quarter of an hour. It was the Frenchman's 18th goal of a stellar season where he'd be crowned joint *capocannoniere* (top goalscorer). That wasn't the title the striker wanted the most though, and with eight minutes remaining in this crucial showdown Igor Tudor scored what looked like a priceless winner that would put the *bianconeri* top of Serie A.

Inter though – and Clarence Seedorf in particular – had other ideas. With the match in added time the Dutchman sent another rocket past Gianluigi Buffon to send the *interisti* into raptures. It was a goal that'd keep Héctor Cúper's men at the top of the table and leave Juventus deflated.

Down in the capital, the reigning champions were about to make a statement in the third derby to take place in as many weeks. The message was that they wouldn't be giving up their title without an almighty fight, as they were about to inflict on Lazio their heaviest derby defeat in almost 70 years. Vincenzo Montella did the damage, scoring an incredible four times before captain Francesco Totti applied the *coup de grâce*, lobbing the hapless Angelo Peruzzi.

Roma were now level at the top with Inter and over the next month it looked like Juventus' hopes of a first scudetto in four seasons were all but over. A narrow win over Verona would be their only win in four matches. A dramatic late defeat at Parma followed by an unimpressive home draw with Lazio left the Turin giants six points off the lead with just five games left – and by their own admission out of the title race.

Within seven days though that advantage was halved as Juventus enjoyed a hugely profitable weekend. First Inter crashed to a shock home defeat against mid-table Atalanta and Roma would fare little better as two late Vincenzo Montella rescued them from defeat at rock-bottom Venezia. Four games to go then and the top three were separated by just three points in a thrilling title race.

Week 31 was equally full of drama. While Roma were cruising to victory over Parma, things were very different for both Inter and Juventus. Two late goals from Ronaldo saw the *nerazzurri* scrape past Brescia – who'd actually taken the lead thanks to a first-half penalty from a certain Pep Guardiola. Juventus meanwhile had the small matter of having to beat Milan to stay in contention for the title, on a day when Carlo Ancelotti was making a first return to Turin since being unceremoniously dumped almost a year earlier. His afternoon would end in disappointment though as José Chamot's own goal midway through the second half proved enough for the *bianconeri* to pick up a priceless three points.

Things got tighter still the following weekend. Federico Cossato's last-gasp equaliser saw Inter held at Chievo and with Roma also only picking up a point, Juventus took full advantage. Pavel Nedvěd's stunning strike was enough for victory at Piacenza. Having seemingly been out of the title race just a few weeks earlier, Marcello Lippi's side were now only a point behind Inter with Roma a further point back.

The penultimate round of the season would see all three cruise to victory. Inter saw off Piacenza at the San Siro while Juventus and Roma would both hit five – against Brescia and Chievo respectively. So, as we headed into the final weekend we incredibly had all three sides in with a shout of the title.

It was a final-day scenario that was almost unheard of (certainly in Channel 4's coverage of Serie A): we had three potential winners on what would prove to be our final day in the decade of *Football Italia* on our screens – and for the fourth year running the title would be decided on the final day. With the channel's commitment to the programme waning over recent years it was obviously disappointing for the entire production that the most thrilling final day we'd ever had wouldn't be shown live. As we headed into it, Inter still boasted that one-point advantage over Juventus with Roma a further point behind.

It really was the day of reckoning for Héctor Cúper's *nerazzurri*. A superb debut season in Italy had the new coach on the brink of earning the club a first scudetto since 1989. City rivals Milan had won five titles in that period so it really felt like it was Inter's moment. There was only one problem – they had by far and away the toughest assignment of the three title contenders on the final day, facing Lazio in the capital, a side still needing a win to have a chance of qualification for the UEFA Cup. Juventus didn't have it that easy though, as they travelled to Udinese. They were equally desperate for the points in their relegation fight. Roma had – on paper at least – the easiest game of the trio, away to a Torino side with nothing to play for.

The Lazio versus Inter clash was all that anybody was talking about though and it wasn't just events on the field that had caught the media's attention. The *laziali* were in a bit of a quandary. Obviously, they wanted to see their side win as that might qualify them for Europe, but the thought of them handing the title to Juventus didn't bear thinking about. Not only that but potentially gifting bitter rivals Roma a second straight scudetto would be the stuff of nightmares.

With the final Sunday almost upon us news broke that Lazio's ultras – the *irrudicibili* – would not be celebrating if their side scored and would instead be cheering for Inter. Not only that, they wanted the fans to come to the game in Inter shirts and bring *nerazzurri* flags and scarves to show where their loyalties lay in these rather unique circumstances. The club had built up a friendship with the *interisti* during the '80s and that was maintained when the sides met in the 1998 UEFA Cup Final – a match in which Inter triumphed 3–0.

This friendship was mainly based on the political views of the ultras. Lazio's have always been far right, and while the *interisti* haven't been as extreme, traditionally have tendencies towards the right too.

Given the drama that was about to unfold, the tension at the Stadio Olimpico was palpable. After 12 minutes Inter struck. Christian Vieri pounced on an uncharacteristic error from ex-Inter and Juventus keeper Angelo Peruzzi. We'd all expected a dramatic afternoon but the first signs of danger for Inter came from Udine with news that both David Trezeguet and Alessandro Del Piero had struck inside the first ten minutes for Juventus to set them up for a routine win. That scoreline would prove fatal for Roma's title dreams, given that they went into the final day a point behind the *bianconeri*.

So, it was all eyes on the Stadio Olimpico as either Inter or Juventus were going to be crowned champions, and within minutes there was stunned silence from the Curva Nord as Karel Poborský smashed home the equaliser to put Juventus in pole position. However, the afternoon would take another dramatic twist within five minutes. Former Roma midfielder Luigi Di Biagio headed home from a corner past Angelo Peruzzi to make it 2–1. It was a goal that would mean more to him than many, given his Roma past.

The celebrations in most of the stadium had only just died down when Poborský hauled Lazio level for a second time. His two goals in the first half had seen him double his tally for the entire season and as half time approached, Inter still had it all to do. With Juventus in the lead in Udine they had to find a winning goal or their title dreams would go up in smoke.

Ten minutes into the second half came the goal that would prove to be the death knell for Inter's title dreams, as former *nerazzurri* midfielder Diego Simeone headed past Francesco Toldo. As a mark of respect, the Argentina international refused to celebrate, and the goal had more than a touch of irony about it. Just a couple of years earlier it had been Simeone who'd scored the priceless winner against Juventus that helped the side from the capital win the title against all the odds, and here he was scoring another hugely important goal that would see Lazio all but hand the title to Juventus.

Simone Inzaghi made it 4–2 with a quarter of an hour to go to hammer down the final nail in the *nerazzurri* coffin, after which Inter boss Héctor Cúper admitted defeat – substituting Ronaldo. Soon after the Brazilian would break down in tears on the Inter bench – a moment which would be the iconic image of the *nerazzurri*'s disastrous afternoon at the Stadio Olimpico. Just a couple of years on from *il fenomeno*'s horrendous injury in the Coppa Italia Final, Ronaldo would be leaving the capital once again in utter devastation.

The Brazilian was inconsolable as the Italian media besieged him after the full-time whistle. "The bitterness [for the defeat] is even greater because we were so close." He went on: "disappointment seems to be my partner in life. In a matter of moments our dreams vanished, overtaken by reality which seems even harder to believe."

Club President Massimo Moratti was more brutal in his assessment of the afternoon. "I am tired, fed up and angry. Today no fan of Inter wants to hear words of consolation and I'm no different." It all meant that Inter had now suffered the longest scudetto drought in their history.

As Gianluca Paparesta blew the final whistle to an almost eerie silence in the capital the contrast couldn't have been greater in the far north-east of Italy, as Juventus claimed their 26th scudetto amid scenes of wild celebration at the Friuli stadium. Marcello Lippi – just three years after his dramatic departure from the club – had achieved the seemingly impossible by winning the scudetto, the one which everyone in Turin had admitted defeat on just a few weeks earlier.

Juventus saw this scudetto as vengeance for the bitter disappointment they'd suffered in Perugia two years earlier, the irony being that it was Lazio – the side who'd pipped the *bianconeri* to the title – who had handed it to them. The *bianconeri* had enjoyed just one week at the Serie A summit all season – now here they were champions of Italy once again, and their joy was beyond measure. This was a scudetto that meant everything to them.

10

END OF AN ERA

There was still one final episode of *Gazzetta Football Italia* to be produced and edited on what had been an emotional week for the entire production team. On a personal level, working on *Football Italia* were without doubt the happiest years of my working career. I spent it surrounded by some truly special people, some of whom are still friends to this day and some who are very sadly no longer with us.

There are three people I want to pay particular tribute to here, all of whom I worked with on the production. I learned so much from all of them in so many ways – especially in my early years on the production. I joined what was then Chrysalis Television aged 19 and I was privileged to work with people whose careers had spanned many decades and who would all offer words of wisdom when needed. Not only that, they all talked to me as an equal, even in my early days as a runner!

Kenneth Wolstenholme

What more can you say of the legendary Kenneth Wolstenholme? The man with the most celebrated commentary line in football, I feel privileged to have known and worked with him. Before I started working on the production I was at my grandfather's house one day when he told me that Ken would be the voice of *Gazzetta*. Despite knowing all about the glorious summer of 1966, to my subsequent shame I didn't realise who Ken was but I would soon learn all about him and get to know the man himself – everything I'd heard rang true.

I first met Ken in the late summer of 1993, when he was in his early '70s. I'd just joined Chrysalis ahead of the second year of coverage and in the rare moments of peace and tranquility during the chaotic *Gazzetta* edit day I would find time to sit down with him and talk about anything and everything. He'd usually show up just before 11.00am and soon after his arrival in the edit suite his bacon sandwich and cup of tea would arrive. Sometimes I'd be editing VTs for the show in the same edit suite and this gave me an opportunity to get distracted; I'd ask Ken about his week. He was always happy to talk about what was going on in his life and what he'd been up to during the week. Ken was a very special man. Given his illustrious career he wasn't just interested in talking about himself, he'd be more than happy (in between looking at his voiceover scripts) to ask others about themselves, and really enjoyed listening to stories, whatever they were about.

His life had certainly not been a run-of-the-mill one. Aged just 19 he became a war hero with the Royal Air Force, flying an incredible 89 raids, during which time he'd racked up almost 1,500 miles. His logbooks from the war told some remarkable stories. He nearly lost his life in 1941 while carrying out a bombing raid over the North Sea. He was with his air observer Sergeant John Wilson, a man nicknamed "Polly".

The logbook read:

> [...] very shaky do. Three shells in nose – one got Polly. Blew half his head away. P [port wing] smashed, tail and elevator riddled. Big shell hole in fin, bomb doors shot away, electrical system shot away, cockpit, belly, both engines riddled with holes. Saw Bob [the pilot of another plane] go down with the engine on fire, made mess of island. Bags of smoke, dust and flame. Hell of a lot of flak. Titch worked like hell on guns. Glad to see West Raynham [RAF base in Norfolk] and land. Drunk that night – thank God!

After the war, he was awarded the Distinguished Flying Cross and Bar in recognition of his "outstanding courage". His heroic bravery during the war had understandably taken its toll and in later years he had no desire to fly as a pilot or a passenger.

Post-war though his broadcasting career really took off, and after joining BBC Radio he soon moved into television. He commentated on the first ever *Match of the Day* as well as every FA Cup Final from 1953 to 1971. His finest hour was of course in the 1966 World Cup Final, as England won the trophy against West Germany after extra time, at the end of which he uttered 14 immortal words which, to this day, are the most famous words in broadcasting history in this country and beyond: "Some people are on the pitch ... They think it's all over ... it is now!"

Several decades later those words were used as the title for a sports quiz show on the BBC. The very idea of the famous line being repeated for the show really upset Ken, who threatened to sue at one point, he was so offended by the flagrant lack of respect the production company had showed him.

Ken's main passion was his beloved Bolton Wanderers. He was born not far from Burnden Park and when I spoke to him he'd always tell stories of his memories of going there from when he was a small child. In 1997, he invited me into the directors' box for the last game at Bolton's iconic stadium; the club were moving to a new stadium in nearby Horwich as they'd just returned to the Premier League.

It was a wonderful night of celebration for the club and it was a privilege and an honour to be there as Bolton took on Charlton Athletic – the team I support. With no pressure at all on either side (Bolton were champions and Charlton in mid-table) the stage was set on a glorious early summer's evening in the north-west. Past players were paraded around the pitch prior to kick-off on a night of celebration and emotion – as the club's 102 years of tradition at Burnden Park was set to come to an end. On the field though things didn't start so well. Charlton stunned the home side as Mark Kinsella fired a first-half rocket past Keith Branagan. It was always going to be Bolton's night though and they blew the visitors away in the second half. Goals from Alan Thompson, Gerry Taggart and two more from the legendary John McGinlay saw the Whites sign off at Burnden Park in style as they received the trophy amid emotional scenes.

His day with us in the edit would be a busy one. After making light work of his breakfast Ken would get to reading the scripts – of which there were plenty. As the main voiceover of not only *Gazzetta* but also the pre-match VTs on *Football Italia*, there was plenty of voicing to be done and although he asked the odd question about pronunciations his grasp of Italian names was pretty impressive. He was a true professional and whatever you threw at him script-wise he could handle it, but there was one occasion when the Italian pronunciations did get the better of him!

One of the scripts he voiced was our goals of the week VT which we ran at half-time during the live game on a Sunday. Unfortunately, the best goal on that particular week was scored by Genoa midfielder Gennaro Ruotolo. Ken just couldn't grasp how to pronounce his name. Retake after retake … he'd struggle with Gennaro but when we got there the surname was another obstacle.

"Rooooootolo?" he'd ask, hoping the torment was over.

"Sorry Ken, it's RU-O-TO-LO!"

We nailed it on take 23 and with all the voicing for *Gazzetta* as well as all the VTs for *Football Italia* done it was almost time for a well-deserved lunch, but not before the infamous RTÉ script. We produced a one-hour highlights show for the Irish state broadcaster on a Monday which featured extended highlights of the second biggest game of the week along with brief highlights of our game with the goals round-up at the end.

Obviously, we needed to cover all bases as we used Ken's voiceover for the show so we had him record links for either side winning, as well as if it was a draw. The script would read something like this:

"So, a great win for Milan to strengthen their title bid …"

"So, a point apiece and a great result for Bari …"

"So, a fantastic win for Bari and a huge setback for Milan's title hopes …"

Ken would call these the "ifs and the buts". They'd be the last thing for him to voice and by the time he'd finished it was time for his well-earned lunch, and what a banquet it was! Ken had the same every week – a prawn and avocado salad – and it was served amid great ceremony with a bottle of chilled white wine.

While he'd be eating (and drinking) he'd ask me lots of questions, and we'd discuss all manner of things regarding both English and Italian football. In those early days of the Premier League, football was starting to become a big business in this country. Ken hated that – he was a real traditionalist and would be far from impressed about what the game has now become! There was usually about enough wine in the bottle for half a glass by the time Ken left, when he'd travel by taxi to his home in Surrey.

He loved a game of golf at the RAC Club in Epsom. He'd certainly more than earned the right to have an enjoyable retirement with his wife Joan. Tragically in the late summer of 1997 Joan passed away following a brain haemorrhage. They'd been childhood sweethearts and tied the knot in Eccles – her birthplace – in 1944. After more than half a century of married bliss the loss of his wife understandably devastated Ken and he moved to Torquay to be near his daughter Lena.

Ken stood down from *Football Italia* just before the production headed to Leeds in 2000, but would make one final appearance on a live game the following season.

He passed away in the spring of 2002. His funeral was held at a crematorium in Surrey and I felt it a privilege to attend. Stars of football and broadcasting past and present were there. I'll never forget the mass of people inside the chapel – dozens who couldn't get seats were standing all around inside and outside, such was the affection people had for Ken.

After the service, we headed to the RAC Club. It was a fitting place to say adieu to a broadcasting legend. From my own perspective, I learned an enormous amount about television in the 1950s and '60s, but more than that I considered Ken to be not just a colleague but a real gentleman. It was a true privilege to get to know him. He was the pinnacle of professionalism and he continues to be sorely missed.

Peter Brackley

Peter Brackley (or "Brackers" as we affectionately called him) was another legend of broadcasting. A proud Sussex man, he was renowned for being a passionate supporter of his local side – Brighton and Hove Albion. He stayed loyal to the club throughout their ground-sharing years at Gillingham and subsequently at the much-maligned Withdean Stadium for over a decade. He'd often come into Channel 4 on a Sunday beaming with pride and singing, usually about the Seagulls' star player: "When the ball hits the goal, it's not Shearer or Cole, it's Zamora!"

Peter's broadcasting career began at BBC Radio Brighton in the 1970s before moving to BBC Radio 2. In those days, the station doubled up as a sports broadcaster and he commentated on two FA Cup Finals as well as the 1982 European Cup Final when Aston Villa triumphed over Bayern Munich. Soon after, Brackers made the move into television with Central Independent Television (part of the ITV network) and would commentate on both the European Championships in 1984 as well as the 1986 World Cup, including the semi-finals of both events.

His career continued its upward curve as he joined ITV and commentated on his first live match for the channel in 1986 for the clash between Manchester United and Sheffield Wednesday, but his lack of progression frustrated him. With Brian Moore, Martin Tyler and Alan Parry all above him in the pecking order, Brackers was on the move again and joined Sky Television, where he'd commentate with Gary Bloom, among others. They would later link up again on Channel 4.

When Sky and BSB merged in 1991 Peter moved on to Italian football and within a year he'd found a new home, as the voice of Sunday afternoons on *Football Italia.* It really was a match made in heaven. He'd worked the previous year on Sky's Serie A coverage and was by now familiar with the league before Channel 4 picked up the rights in 1992. I'd like to think he spent some of the happiest years of his career on our programmes.

The production was one of the first of its kind not to have commentators at the game. We obviously had an on-site presence with James Richardson and a pundit, but very few people genuinely believed he wasn't at the game.

He was a consummate professional. His commentary notes were something to behold, there wasn't an inch of the page that wasn't covered in all manner of colours. He only appeared on our screens once in the decade we were on air when he acted as a jovial barman at the Chrysalis Television Christmas party, cracking jokes while he served customers. When he wasn't commentating, comedy was what he was all about and he had a great talent – whether he was doing impressions or taking the mickey out of someone.

After famously standing in as the voice for Jimmy Greaves on *Saint and Greavsie*, it was clear that he had the ability to be a top impressionist but he was also very talented and quick-witted too. If anyone made the slightest mistake or stumbled on something, Brackers would pounce on them quick as a flash. It didn't matter whether it was in the green room or on air. His comedic style made him hugely popular among the production team and our ever-increasing viewership.

It was on *Football Italia* that Brackers' on-air rapport with former Milan midfielder Ray Wilkins took off. The chemistry between them was so natural. We tried to ensure Ray was booked as much as possible because of what he added to the show and in particular his seemingly telepathic relationship with Brackers. Whether it was his receding hairline or to do with his height, Ray was more often than not on the receiving end of Brackers' light-hearted humour. Whenever there was a break in play he'd ask about his playing, or in later years coaching career, and Ray would go into great detail as to what was going on, sometimes even behind the scenes. They were the perfect match and while we had a wealth of co-commentators we could call upon and Brackers was always a complete professional, the comedy edge just wasn't there with anybody else. Ray wasn't just a co-commentator, he was a key cog in the production who was valued by all.

Brackers had opinions on everything; he certainly wasn't what you'd call a reserved character. One of my roles when I started out as a runner was to bring the food for everyone's lunch. This would involve going around Tesco and coming to Channel 4 with about six hefty bags of sandwiches, drinks, fruit, crisps, chocolate and endless cans of beer for watching the Premier League match once we were off air. In those days, I didn't drive so to get all the bags from Tesco to work would involve taking a supermarket trolley and then leaving it just around the corner from Channel 4. It would never be there the following week but it was a regimented process on a weekly basis.

There were all sorts of complaints when I arrived in the green room:

"Why aren't there any chicken sandwiches?"

"There's only beef or that disgusting-looking thing, there needs to be more variety!"

"I don't like Twixes, can you get Kit Kats next week?"

"You should get freshly made sandwiches, these have all been frozen."

"These beers are disgusting – can you get Carling next week please?"

First-world problems. Brackers had his own request though. "Could I just have some crusty rolls and a packet of turkey please? I cannot stand all the crap they put in sandwiches – why can't they just make it simple?"

Here was a man who liked the simple things in life, he told me what he wanted, it was crystal clear ... why aren't they all like this? The truth was that the selection wasn't that extensive on a Sunday, but my excuses invariably fell on deaf ears. As long as Brackers had his turkey rolls, I knew I'd have his support!

One aspect of his life that he treasured was his apartment near Málaga in Spain. He used to escape the grey, wet English winter and enjoy the sunshine there during the week. While we all staggered to work in driving rain or the arctic cold during the winter months Brackers would breeze in fresh as a daisy.

"How are you, Pete? Good week?"

"Really lovely thanks, been to Spain – 75 degrees every day..."

That was a conversation-stopper. The short, depressingly grey days of November and December didn't affect Brackers at all. He just jumped on a plane and spent the week on the beach!

I was always desperately keen to keep him happy. If we were covering a lesser-known team that we wouldn't normally feature live he'd ask me to record about half an hour of a recent match of theirs onto a VHS tape so could familiarise himself with the players and their formation before we went on air. His knowledge of the league, however, was second to none and I'm sure he didn't really need the tapes. It was a security blanket for him but he knew the players anyway.

The move to Leeds was less than ideal for him though, commuting as he was from Brighton. He didn't enjoy the long trip to Yorkshire each week and was frustrated by the fact the sound mix wasn't as good as we'd had at Channel 4. He came in one day with two tapes. One recorded in London and one in Leeds ... "Listen to that, you can't compare them! Why can't they get the mix as good as at Channel 4? It sounds tinny, it sounds dreadful!"

Whatever I said wasn't going to cut it. We both wanted the production to be back in London. I was travelling down the M1 for a couple of days at home as it was each week. It just wasn't possible though. Channel 4 had made this a regional production and we just had to get on with it.

As it transpired, he was only in Leeds for one season anyway. *La Partita* would be with us for the final year of the contract and he would be back to working in London on a Sunday, and when the season ended amid tears for Inter it was an emotional farewell for all of us.

While he was still busy commentating on domestic and international football, the end of *Football Italia* must have been tough for him, as it was for us all. I was made redundant a few months after it all ended before moving into freelancing.

Unfortunately, I lost touch with Peter a few years after we came off the air until I received a very worrying text from a former work colleague on *Football Italia.* It said that Peter was seriously ill. He'd suffered a suspected heart attack two years earlier and had suffered some equally serious cardiac issues. On 14 October 2018 he sadly passed away, aged 67.

I have nothing but happy and positive memories of Brackers. He was always the beaming, jovial face of our live Sunday games. I miss him as a person, his larger-than-life sense of humour and his ability to bring so much happiness and joy to a room. This is something I will always remember.

Tom Docherty

There's one other member of our production team who sadly passed away in 2016 that I wanted to pay tribute to. Programme director Tom Docherty was someone who I got very close to as the years went by and I learned a vast amount about live production from him. Early on I found working in television very daunting and intimidating – it's an industry where you have to be pretty thick-skinned. I have found in other productions I've worked on to have groups of people (mainly at a senior level) to socialise in cliques. There was none of that on *Football Italia.*

Tom was director of the live shows throughout our decade of coverage and would be series editor of *La Partita* during our final year on Channel 4. I first met him in 1993 and was immediately struck by the fact he was always willing to offer advice, for which I was especially grateful. In later years I would discover this was far from the norm. Tom had worked for the biggest broadcasters in the country on some high-level programmes, his experience was vast and he had more than a few stories to tell. Every so often he might have a small bet on a sporting event – and he once told me the story of when he was covering one of the many snooker championships he was employed on and there was a big match involving the late Alex Higgins. The man known as "Hurricane" was up against it during a match and, during a break in play when he was staring down the barrel of a heavy defeat, told Tom to put a bet on him to win at what were naturally very long odds. Needless to say, he made a Lazarus-like recovery and pocketed (no pun intended) Tom a tidy sum.

While he wasn't a gambler he did like a small bet every now and then and he would always text me if he'd had a good result betting-wise. On Boxing Day in 2011 I was driving to my mother's place and my team – Charlton – were top of League One and trailing to Yeovil in what looked like being a huge upset. Two late goals saw Charlton win 3–2 and lo and behold I get a text from Tom a couple of days later, featuring a screenshot of his bet. Charlton to win 3–2 at 20/1! Quite how anyone could have predicted that was beyond me.

I got a lot closer to Tom as the years passed to the extent that we would regularly text each other about all manner of things. When Charlton finally reached the Premier League I obviously invited him to come with me to see them play Manchester United at The Valley. Tom was a huge United fan and he remarked on the way in how much he loved the walk to the stadium and the ground itself. In this new age of modern soulless stadia, he was struck by the fact that here was a traditional old-fashioned community stadium and it was like going back in time to when football wasn't the money machine it has become.

Charlton's eight-year stay in the top flight would see me invite him every season (one year we even managed to wangle our way in the directors' box), but in 1999 we had a fight on our hands to get to the game. It was a 4.00pm kick-off on a Sunday and we'd come off air on *Football Italia* at 3.30pm. We agreed beforehand that we'd make the swiftest of getaways and if we missed the first 15 minutes or more, then so be it. What followed was quite remarkable, as we raced along the Embankment, past Tower Bridge, through the Blackwall Tunnel to be in our seats by ten past four. The match had kicked off late so I think we only missed the first five minutes! It was Tom who would leave happier as Dwight Yorke headed in an 89th-minute winner as United headed for the title, and Charlton for relegation.

It wasn't just on *Football Italia* that we worked together. Chrysalis Sport (my employer – now known as North One Television) had been commissioned to broadcast some random football matches from around Europe for a whole variety of channels and Tom was booked to direct them. I think it was the one and only time I've ever actually been running adverts from VT! For some unknown reason the gallery was completely overcrowded and Tom was less than impressed as he was actually directing from the back row! As we ran what felt like endless commercials and movie trailers, we looked at each other as if to say "what on earth is going on here?" Safe to say from that day forward the word "Taxi" (a name of one of the movie trailers which looked decidedly second-rate) turned into a long-running joke.

Football Italia was where we worked the majority of our time together and whether we were in the gallery or if I was on talkback in an edit, the jovial banter was always there. One season it was decided that we should run a player of the match VT which involved a shot of whoever it was run as an underlay for the chat between James and our pundit. Said pundit would give me the heads up as to who it would be, and depending on their decisiveness I'd be told who it was a few minutes before the match ended.

Obviously, I'd invariably guessed as to who it might be (some weeks it'd be obvious), and I would make notes on my log of the match and find the shot of the correct player so that could be ticked off as there was also analysis to edit in those days, as well as the closer.

Early in the 1998/99 season we were covering eventual champions Milan away to Serie A new boys Salernitana and after a slow start Milan went 2–0 ahead during the second half thanks to goals from Oliver Bierhoff and Leonardo. With three or four minutes to go, I was given my player of the match expecting it to be one of Milan's stars. How wrong was I! For some reason Salernitana midfielder Roberto Breda was the choice and as I trawled through the match I could not find any shots of him anywhere. With the match about to enter added time and things getting increasingly frantic in my edit, up stepped the aforementioned Breda to curl home a delightful free kick and solve my problems! "There's your shot of Breda!" boomed Tom down talkback. He knew exactly why there was so much silence my end.

It was on the production that Tom met Rachel Clark. She also worked on the programme and they would later get married, spending many happy years together. Rachel was as sharp-witted as Tom and the two of them were a great partnership both as a couple and in a live gallery.

The staunch Manchester United fan that he was, Tom never warmed to the idea of heading to Leeds once the production was made regional at the turn of the millennium. We had a few teething troubles regarding getting staff and talent to Leeds each Sunday so over the first five or six weeks Tom, Peter Brackley and a few others would be booked for the night into a local hotel. I'd actually stayed there for a few nights while I was looking for accommodation for myself and my wife. There was nothing wrong with the hotel – it wasn't too grand (understandably with the ever-shrinking *Football Italia* budget) but the rooms were tiny. Every week I'd arrange to meet Tom and Peter in the hotel bar on a Saturday evening and I'd ask Tom what his room was like.

"Yes, it's another one of the cat-swinging variety", he would say. I think (just like Brackers) the whole Leeds experience wasn't the dream ticket for Tom. Eventually he'd travel up and back to London on the day. He was quite accustomed to train travel as he didn't drive much and most weeks went to visit his young daughter in Manchester. Virgin Trains' service (or lack thereof) was often talked about on a Sunday. I did tease Tom one week about a commercial I had seen during the week, which had the tagline "Business brains take Virgin trains!" He wasn't having it though – endless delays, dire food and exorbitant prices made the experience fairly exhausting for him. One week he mentioned he'd taken his daughter to the cinema.

"What did you see?" We asked.

"*Spiceworld – The Movie*!" It had been a good 72 hours and poor Tom still looked traumatised.

As with Brackers, the Leeds experience lasted only a year and in the final twelve months of the contract Tom oversaw our highlights show *La Partita,* which he produced with his customary talent, expertise and professionalism. Our working paths didn't really cross again but we always kept in touch and I was proud to not just call him a colleague but a friend. In fact, I still work with his wife Rachel on a variety of productions.

We kept in touch fairly regularly once *Football Italia* came off the air and during the programme's short renaissance on Bravo we worked together again. But after that it was mainly by phone or text that we kept in touch, there'd be plenty of jokes fired backwards and forwards. We got each other's sense of humour really well.

By the end of 2015 I didn't really have much communication with Tom. I kept meaning to call him but having kids of my own and with work commitments I never got around to it and really regret it. In the

New Year, in a rare quiet moment, I logged onto my social media account and saw some quite cryptic messages from people saying how they worked with him and how upset they were. I tried to tell myself that it couldn't be true and then I saw a message from a work colleague to say how devastated they were about never seeing or working with him again. I then saw a picture of her and Tom in a gallery that had been posted as a tear rolled down my cheek. The next day I got the text from Rachel with the awful news.

Tom had been admitted to hospital just before Christmas. He passed away in mid-January with Rachel by his side, aged just 59. Rachel asked me to read Tom's favourite poem – *Funeral Blues* by W.H. Auden. I stood at the lectern hugely honoured to be asked, given the sheer volume of people present, took a breath and tried to maintain my composure. The service was incredibly poignant and emotional with so many of his work colleagues past and present telling stories of Tom. I still desperately miss him to this day and haven't deleted his number on my telephone. I want to hold on to those memories.

When I look back at the *Football Italia* years it does now seem a lifetime ago. We've lost three of the biggest stars of the production, as well as Ray Wilkins. One of the reasons I wanted to write the book wasn't just to bring back memories of this golden age of Italian football to the reader but also to pay tribute to those three people who'd had an enormous impact on my working life.

I was full of emotion, recalling a time when football was very different. Although there were a few signs of it becoming the money machine it is today, it wasn't about the financial rewards as much as it is now. You had players like Francesco Totti and Alessandro Del Piero. Both were captains, symbols of their clubs – and while they among others were handsomely remunerated they both achieved immortality in the supporters' eyes by staying loyal, becoming one-club players. There are few – if any – examples of this in the modern game, which illustrates the way football has changed.

If you watch a Premier League game, for example, you'll see players being paid hundreds of thousands of pounds per week, some of whom won't start regularly even if they're 100% fit. Some of them are frustrated and stir up trouble through their agents, which is disappointing. Others have the attitude of not being that bothered about playing at all, as long as they're earning hugely over-inflated wages they're seemingly happy to let their playing careers drift.

Back in 2002 this wasn't as much of an issue as it is today. Looking back to the end of our coverage, while it was (for me at least) quite emotional after working on a production for almost a decade it felt that the timing was right. Serie A – and Italy in general – was no longer home to the cream of European football. No Italian side had made it to the Champions League Final since 1998 and no Italian side had tasted success in the competition since Juventus in 1996. The UEFA Cup (or Europa League as it's now known) was a similar story. After Italian sides had won it six times in seven years in the '90s there hadn't been any Italian representation in the final since 1999.

Two of Serie A's big guns of the '90s had also been beset by financial problems and were in serious trouble. As well as the aforementioned Fiorentina, Parma were also in dire straits. The club had been one of the Cinderella stories of the decade, finally arriving in Italy's top flight in 1990 under the club's legendary coach Nevio Scala and winning titles both at home and in Europe. The investment came from local food processing company Parmalat – a global giant that was founded by Calisto Tanzi. Throughout the '90s Parmalat would invest hugely in the club as international stars – Zola, Asprilla, Cannavaro, Thuram, Crespo and Chiesa to name but a few – would all ply their trade at the Ennio Tardini stadium.

Under Scala, Carlo Ancelotti and later Alberto Malesani, the titles would keep on coming – two Italian Cups and an Italian Super Cup. Parma would also be hugely successful on the continent too, winning the Cup Winners' Cup as well as the European Super Cup. They were also victorious in the UEFA Cup twice. But by the time the new millennium came things started to change, and Parma were unable to match the fees that some of the big guns would pay. It was the beginning of a slow regression for the club and in the summer of 2004 it was declared insolvent following the financial meltdown of Parmalat. The company had a €14 billion hole in their accounts, in what remains Europe's biggest bankruptcy. Tanzi was found guilty of embezzling an estimated €800 million from the company and was jailed.

Parma would be liquidated and re-formed as Parma Football Club SpA. Their golden era was at an end and before long they'd be relegated to Serie B. The club would rise again though under new ownership and while the days since have seen stability both on and off the field the era of multi-million pound transfers are over. They are now a well-run club and while Parma are among the established names in Italy's top flight they are a long way off the pace of the big guns of Serie A. This was illustrated by the standings at the end of 2019/20 campaign, which saw the club finish almost 30 points adrift of the final Champions League qualifying place.

11

FINAL REFLECTIONS

The demise of Parma and Fiorentina back in 2002 was symptomatic of the state of Italian football at the time and it wasn't just on the field that Serie A had lost its way. As previously mentioned, Italian sides were by now failing to make an impression in European competition. The days of Serie A dominance were a distant memory.

Off the field things had turned pretty grim too. Crowd violence was sadly evident and even more disappointingly there was racism too. Having witnessed Juventus play Lazio in 2000, it was shocking to listen to. Edgar Davids' every touch was greeted with monkey noises from the *laziali*. The club's fans' racism would be even more prominent over the coming years.

It wasn't just racism that was a problem though. Violence had become evident too. The senseless murder of Vincenzo Spagnolo back in 1995 was just the start of it for our *Football Italia* viewers who would sometimes see policemen with truncheons entering ultras territory in Italian stadiums as well as seats being set on fire, but in 2001 things reached a new low when some hardcore Inter fans threw that Vespa from the upper tier of the San Siro. It was a deeply troubled season for the *nerazzurri* – a campaign which had seen them thrashed 6–0 by arch rivals Milan as well as receiving a stadium ban for another offence.

It wasn't just off the field that things had turned sour though. While results in European competition were on the slide, the league itself was in the new millennium becoming a shadow of its former self, as the Premier League and La Liga were now seen as the best divisions in Europe. Attendances were starting to fall and the world's biggest talent were no longer being drawn to Italy. The big transfers of the new millennium weren't to Serie A clubs. As our contract ended, the league was a pale shadow of what it had been a decade earlier. After being seen as the greatest league in the world during the '90s, finances were now a problem. The demise of Parma and Fiorentina were a clear illustration of that.

In October 2002 – around five months after we came off the air and after a fair old while twiddling my thumbs in the office – I went into a meeting with the company hierarchy to be told I was being made redundant. I went into freelancing as my journey on *Football Italia* had come to an end, but I'd enjoyed a lifetime of memories and forged friendships with members of our production team.

I said at the start of this book that the years spent on the *Football Italia* production were the happiest working days of my television career. In the mid-'90s the risk assessment forms that are on all productions weren't as rigorous and still bring a smile to my face. The fact that we had a shoot with Gazza at a wildlife park with a snake around his neck just wouldn't happen these days. We also filmed a link when he had his fingers on a fence and we had to scream at him to move them as a tiger was approaching. His response? "Jeez, thought it had bit us there!"

So many memories. Getting Gianluca Vialli to wear a wig, putting Paul Ince in a chicken costume, getting David Platt to tear around the corner of his driveway in his car, screeching to a halt with a cigar in his mouth, before proceeding to grab James by the throat and saying "I'll be back" in true Arnold Schwarzenegger style... There was also the time we had Gazza talking while his head was inside a huge Easter egg – another hilarious moment. The ideas that some of my bosses came up with were truly inspirational.

At the end of it all I look back on the ten years we were on the air on Channel 4 and ask myself what had we achieved? How had the programme evolved and what difference had it made to football fans as well as Channel 4's viewers. The reaction of people I speak to and read about online to this day speaks volumes. It had a cult following.

People knew *Gazzetta Football Italia* was on every Saturday at 10.00am and would watch it religiously. It was the start of the football weekend for fans of the game and I don't think it has ever been truly replaced.

We brought live football to fans who didn't want to fork out for a Sky subscription and for pretty much all of our years on air it was the best live football in the world. We brought the stars of the game into people's living rooms on a Sunday afternoon and viewers of all generations loved it.

So yes, I hope we made a difference and I hope everyone enjoyed it. It was a true honour working on it. They say memories fade with time but for me they won't. It might have been a job but to me it felt like so much more.

That car journey with my father back in 1992 has led to a lifetime of memories, and they are all happy ones. For me, the world of Italian football will always be a beautiful one and the impact it's had on my life will last forever. Working on *Football Italia* was a dream job for me – quite why they called it "work" I'll never know.

ACKNOWLEDGEMENTS

There are so many people to thank for their help – from the beginning in 1992 to the present day.

I'll start with my family for their belief and support. They've been there every step of the way. What started as an idea has developed into this book which I hope has given you a flavour of what it was like behind the scenes, as well as recalling a time full of great memories.

I also owe a huge debt of gratitude to the team I worked with during our decade of Serie A coverage. My bosses Neil Duncanson and Steve Gowans gave someone with very little television experience a chance, and I owe so much to them both. As I said in the book, the days working on *Football Italia* were among the most enjoyable in my career.

I also must pay tribute to our presenter James Richardson, who throughout our time on air was a pleasure to work with. His sheer professionalism – not to mention his incredibly sharp sense of humour – was key to the incredible success of the show.

While some of my former colleagues are sadly no longer with us, they helped create a lifetime of memories, and I am sure I speak for the entire team when I say they will never be forgotten.

I also want to thank my editor Michelle Tilling for her tireless work in helping me with the publication of this book – her assistance has been invaluable.

Finally, I want to thank you – the viewers. It was a pleasure and an honour working on our programmes. I hope you enjoyed them just as much.

Jonathan Grade
November 2020

Printed by Amazon Italia Logistica S.r.l.
Torrazza Piemonte (TO), Italy

16209500R00103